I'LL DRINK TO THAT!

I'LL DRINK TO THAT!

Broadway's Legendary Stars, Classic Shows,
and the Cocktails They Inspired

LAURENCE MASLON

*Cocktail Photography
by Joan Marcus*

weldon**owen**

CONTENTS

PREVIOUS SPREAD Just sensational: Angela Lansbury as *Mame* (1966).

CHAPTER FOUR

Faraway Places: Where the Sky Meets the Sea

THE HEATHER ON THE HILL • DEFYING GRAVITY •
THE DEAD THING • THE BALI HA'I MA'I TA'I

CHAPTER FIVE

Watering Holes: Right This Way, Your Table's Waiting

THE HAMILTON SHOT • THE L'CHAIM • THE BLOODY SWEENEY •
BEWITCHED, BOTHERED, AND BEWILDERED • THE TOAST OF MAYFAIR •
THE LUCKY LADY AND THE BELLRINGER • THE TURKEY LURKEY

CHAPTER SIX

Show Queens: Here's to the Ladies!

MAME'S MINT JULEP • THE SAZERAC • THE ANNIE WARBUCKS •
THE PINK LADY • THE LOVERLY • RAINBOW HIGH

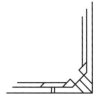

INTRODUCTION

When I first saw the musical *On the Twentieth Century* from a mezzanine seat at the Colonial Theatre during its 1978 Boston tryout, I remember the beginning of the second act, when four tap-dancing porters emerge in front of a vibrant Art Deco backdrop and profess that "life is like a train": there's always light at the end of the tunnel, there's always something new round the bend. In the skilled hands of lyricists Betty Comden and Adolph Green, I found this simile rather persuasive.

Is a cocktail like a Broadway show? Well, they both rely on a combination of volatile ingredients mixed together with grace and delicacy. They're often greater than the sum of their parts. They can be heady, effervescent, and intoxicating. They tend to be better at the end of a long day, and they both exist to make our quotidian existence just a little more exciting.

This book attempts to weave together the connection that Broadway and cocktails have had for more than a century. It measures out into two parts, really: the first is a breezy history of how liquor has found its way onstage (and sometimes offstage) in various Broadway plays and musicals over the last 120 years. The second part is a complementary set of recipes for various cocktails, each of which is inspired in some way or another by an event or a show or a personality in the history of Broadway. (And they're stunningly shot by the best theater photographer of our generation, Joan Marcus, at the archetypical second-floor bar of Sardi's, no less.) One might consider the first part of each chapter as a gentle lecture by a bemused professor, while the second part is a series of anecdotes rendered by a conversant bartender.

There's a theater anecdote about a not-so-great actor in the nineteenth century named George Frederick Cooke—although this story might well have been based on any number of second-rate actors throughout history. Cooke supposedly said once in despair, "I gave a performance on Thursday night drunk and they booed me. I gave a performance Friday night sober and they booed me. What the devil *do* they want?" So, although this book refers many roistering theater folk and their bibulous way of life, I ask readers to take these profiles of mixology in scale and responsibly. This book by no means endorses excessive drinking of alcohol nor behaving in an obstreperous or obnoxious fashion.

In other words, don't do anything the characters in a Noël Coward play wouldn't do.

HOW TO USE THIS BOOK

In creating this book, I had a vision that the reader might get together a group of friends and collaborators after the performance or an opening night of a particular play or musical mentioned herein and throw a civilized cocktail party celebrating its achievement. One might mix a batch of the appropriate cocktail and hoist a glass or two, while sharing a few of the anecdotes mentioned in the book: a kind of themed cocktail party for grown-ups.

With that in mind, I have some thoughts about how this book can best be used.

The first is pretty simple: have fun. The fine art of mixology and the current availability of numerous products that were formerly quite obscure and difficult to find have made creating cocktails an increasingly precise and sometimes rarefied experience. In my opinion, mixing cocktails in the comfort of your own home should not feel like a day's work in a research laboratory, any more than an evening out in the theater should feel like five weeks of technical rehearsal. Please don't be intimidated by any of the suggestions contained in these pages; this isn't rocket science, and no one's life is at stake here. Although my superb editor insists on precise measurements, I think the reader should be allowed to bend the rules a little if they feel so inclined or inspired. You prefer a little more bourbon and a little less vermouth? Go for it.

Many of the recipes are original, inspired by a particular show; some are "improvs" based on a classic; and a couple are simple classics—but they all reflect the taste of the author. There are certain brands of liquor and certain kinds of cocktails I like more than others, and I've recommended these when appropriate. But, if the price range is within your comfort zone, go out and buy something you've never tried before; the worst that can happen is you'll pour the concoction down the drain and hide the bottle behind the sour apple schnapps at the back of the liquor cabinet. The history of Broadway is littered with marvelous musical numbers cut out of town or fantastically imaginative scenery left in the stage door alley after the second preview. As Cole Porter wrote: "The future can offer you infinite joy / And merriment. / Experiment /And you'll see."

Cocktails should also not be as high-priced as house seats for the latest smash musical hit, especially if they are prepared at home for the amusement and entertainment of friends and family. In other words, don't shell out a lot of money for a particular bottle of liquor. Here's a little secret: an expensive bottle of bourbon won't make your Manhattan taste any better. In fact, the various mixtures of different elements into a cocktail mitigate against any singular or expensive taste standing out. There are many wonderful brands to be had on a mid-priced budget. Again, cocktails shouldn't be intimidating; they're just drinks, not a Tom Stoppard trilogy about Russian literary life in the nineteenth century, for Pete's sake.

Once upon a time, Broadway was geared to sending those audience members who wished to do so out to a neighboring bar to enjoy a quick drink during intermission. Anyone who remembers and cherishes the original film of Mel Brooks's *The Producers* (and I hope that's everyone who reads this book) will remember when Zero Mostel and Gene Wilder retire to a neighboring bar and overhear the enthusiastic intermission crowd crow, "Did you ever think you would love a show called *Springtime for Hitler?*" Drinks are now prohibitively expensive in the theaters themselves and no longer limited to the lobby bar. In the English theater, you can order your drink ahead of time and simply pick it up during the interval, which strikes me as

---

THE ICEMAN COMETH

Here's the best piece of advice I can give anyone who wishes to throw a sophisticated cocktail party: always get more ice than you need. However much ice you think you need, buy twice as much. This way you can chill your glasses, too, and, even better, you can make mistakes without running—or stressing—out.

much more civilized and certainly more efficient because you can finish your drink before the second act curtain goes up. (I profess to being rather annoyed by the branded plastic cups that audiences now bring in for the second act; they then invariably rattle their ice cubes at exactly the moment the heroine launches into her big musical number.)

So, to save yourself the aggravation, gather a few chums over to your penthouse apartment, either before or after the theater, and try out a few of these cocktail recipes. You don't even need an excuse: it's today!

BRUSH UP YOUR SHAKES

Cocktail shakers are an essential part of making a cocktail—certainly, as Tom Cruise could tell you, the most theatrical part. At home, most folks can use a cobbler shaker (three parts: bottom, cap, and a middle part with built-in strainer) admirably. A Boston shaker is only two parts, a glass bottom so you can see your handiwork and a metal top, which simply pops on at an angle and, improbably, stays in place. It requires more flamboyant shaking and a separate strainer, which may be better if you are muddling ingredients such as mint or berries. For how long do you shake your cocktail? If you sing (at tempo): "Brush up your Shakespeare / Start quoting him now / Brush up your Shakespeare / And the women you will wow. / Just declaim a few lines from *Othella* / And they think you're a hell of a fella," you should be in good shape to pour.

LEFT The most famous intermission drink sequence in Broadway history is actually from a movie: Mel Brooks's *The Producers*. Here, Gene Wilder and Zero Mostel get some unexpected feedback during intermission of *Springtime for Hitler*.

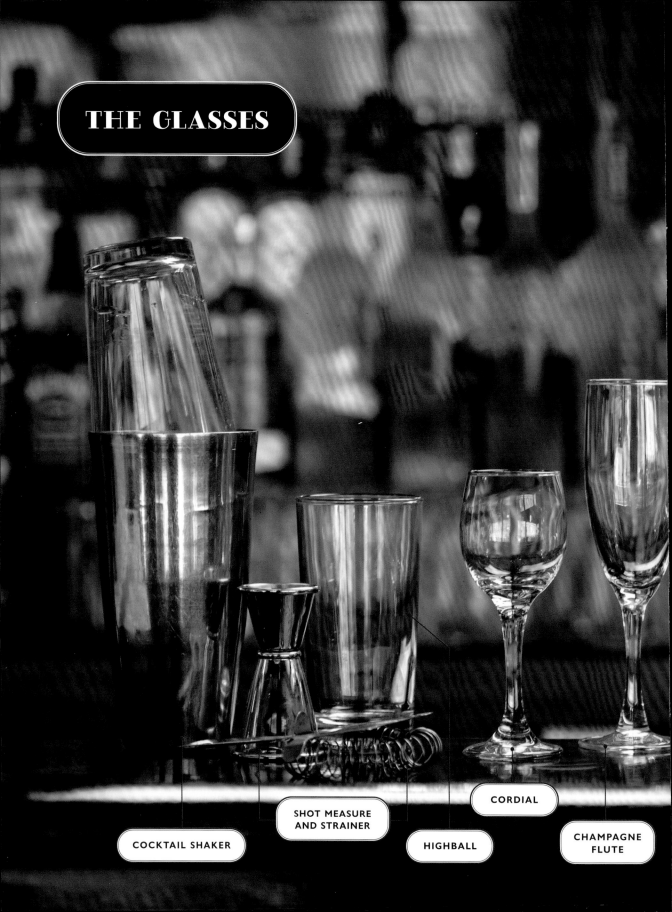

THE GLASSES

COCKTAIL SHAKER

SHOT MEASURE
AND STRAINER

HIGHBALL

CORDIAL

CHAMPAGNE
FLUTE

MARTINI

LOWBALL /
TUMBLER

BRANDY
SNIFTER

COUPE

CHAPTER 1
Champagne

THEY'RE ALWAYS
POPPING THEIR CORK

◇

MIKE *(looking at the Champagne glass)*: That is funny stuff. I'm used to
whiskey. Whiskey is a clap on the back. Champagne, entwining arms.
—*The Philadelphia Story*, **Philip Barry (1939)**

It's hard to say whether Champagne has a more effervescent life onstage or offstage on Broadway. Certainly the "funny stuff" has proved propitious for a celebratory event in numerous plays and musicals. When the actual opening night of a show rolls around, the corks are popped and the glasses raised and the toasts are proclaimed—that is, until a bad review in the *New York Herald-Tribune* gets read aloud. . . .

Champagne's utility as a factotum devoted to all sorts of celebration is an extension of its peculiar history, its uniqueness as a sparkling wine, and a determined public relations campaign stretching back centuries. First things first: champagne isn't always Champagne—or is it the other way around? There are multiple sparkling wines produced around the world—including cava from Spain, prosecco in Italy—but since 1927 only the wines cultivated in the Champagne region of France, located about two hours' drive east of Paris, are allowed to be called Champagne. Of course, that's never stopped folks from using the term to refer to all bubbly wines in a generic fashion.

The miraculous evolution of Champagne is a long story for another time. Suffice it to say that initially—in the late Renaissance—the fermentation of certain wines, conditioned by certain atmospheric changes, created a sparkling beverage that frequently caused thinly bottled wines to, yes, pop their corks and sometimes even explode on their own. Refinements in fermentation continued throughout the sixteenth and seventeenth centuries, and by the end of the eighteenth century, the heady brew was enjoyed and quaffed by the crown heads of Europe and their courtiers. They were, perhaps it can be said, the first "influencers." Major vintners or "houses" in the Champagne district—Moët et Chandon, Piper-Heidsieck, Louis Roederer, Veuve Clicquot—exploited that kind of exalted cachet and the firms quickly pivoted to promoting Champagne as a luxury drink for the middle and upper classes, even getting artists such as Toulouse-Lautrec to create advertisements for their wares. Soon, the wine became a synonym for sophisticated tastes and celebrations, and exalted personalities as varied as Winston Churchill and Marilyn Monroe extolled the virtues of Champagne to the general populace. Now, at the beginning of the twenty-first century, more than 200 million bottles are sold annually.

PREVIOUS SPREAD Lily Garland (played here by Kristen Chenoweth in the 2011 revival of *On the Twentieth Century*) has to chose between two choice stage roles: Mary Magdalene or Babette, the idol of the idle rich. Which do you think she chooses?
RIGHT In the stage version of Philip Barry's *The Philadelphia Story* (1939), Katharine Hepburn as the glacial heiress Tracy Lord dives into a bottle of Pommery to prove that, despite her father's impression, she is not made of bronze.

THE NIGHT THEY INVENTED CHAMPAGNE

It was a simple but obvious innovation for these winemakers to spread a little cash to interpolate "Champagne" into the wider canvas of popular culture and entertainment—the word appears in the lyrics of popular songs as early as the mid-nineteenth century. *Champagne Sec* seemed an attractive title for the 1933 Broadway version of *Die Fledermaus*, in a kind of "user-friendly" musical theater version: operetta lite. Kitty Carlisle had her first real hit playing the showy part of Prince Orlofsky (traditionally played by a woman), and it led directly to a film contract. During rehearsals, she made friends with an ambitious young Viennese composer wannabe who was playing piano in the pit: Frederick Loewe. "One day," he told Carlisle, "I will wrrrrite the grrrreatest musical on Broadway." Kitty patted his hand gently and smiled at him with benevolence.

A quarter-of-a-century later, Loewe and his lyrical partner, Alan Jay Lerner, did, in fact, write the grrrreatest musical on Broadway, *My Fair Lady* (directed by the man who would become Carlisle's husband, Moss Hart). Lerner and Loewe followed up their triumph with the 1958 film *Gigi*, which was not only based on an earlier stage play but would also reappear in its theatrical form on Broadway in 1973 (and again in 2016). In one climactic and highly memorable scene, the teenaged Gigi is playing cards with her family friend, the dashing Gaston. Her grandmother opens a bottle of Champagne:

GIGI: May I have a glass of Champagne, Grandmama?

MAMITA: Are you losing your mind? Of course, you may not!

Well, inevitably, Gigi inveigles Gaston into taking her and her Grandmama to Trouville for the weekend and they rhapsodize their happiness by comparing it to the night that Champagne was invented and waltzing around the living room. "The Night They Invented Champagne" may well be the most famous song ever written about the bubbly—it's certainly one of the bubbliest.

Ironically, the song has been appropriated as extolling a celebratory moment so immense that the Champagne must be broken out, but in the original context, it promises nothing of the sort. Gaston is coming over the house to play cards and relax, so—Oh, those French!—Mamita simply breaks out the Champagne. Why not?

ANOTHER OP'NIN', ANOTHER SHOW

Of course, due to its celebratory nature, Champagne makes a cameo appearance in innumerable backstage plays and musicals—Moss Hart's *Light Up the Sky*, Terrence McNally's *It's Only a Play*, Mel Brooks's *The Producers*—during opening night shenanigans. Nothing, however, can compare with its supporting role in real-life opening nights. Famed restaurant owner Vincent Sardi Jr. had a unique perspective:

> **It's funny about opening nights. There are two distinct tempos after an opening. The first is when the audience arrives in Sardi's after the curtain with a buzz of excitement, which reaches a climax as the featured players, then the stars, enter, each one getting an ovation.**

On March 2, 1927, a play by the revered Italian author Luigi Pirandello opened on Broadway: a Theatre Guild production entitled *Right You Are (If You Think You Are)*. It ran 48 performances and made a star out of a thirty-four-year-old actor named Edward G. Robinson. It's not known exactly where the opening night party was held, but it might well have happened at a restaurant on 44th Street that had its own opening the evening before: Sardi's.

PREVIOUS SPREAD In the original 1958 film *Gigi*, "The Night They Invented Champagne" became an instant anthem for the sparkling wine. A Broadway version in 1973 was the first adaptation of a film musical for the stage; this version (Vanessa Hudgens, Victoria Clark, and Corey Cott) appeared in 2013.

RIGHT In *Les Misérables*, there's nothing like a bottle of brandy (or two) to fortify yourself before fortifying the barricades: call it "French courage."

For almost a century, denizens of the Theater District have operated under a simple equation: Sardi's + opening nights = an event. Founded as a restaurant for theater folk (in a building owned by the Shubert brothers, Broadway's mightiest producing team) by Eugenia and Vincent Sardi, Sardi's is, in many ways, Broadway's longest running show. Stars of the stage rub elbows with tourists from Dubuque, sampling manicotti and chef's salad, encircled by the hundreds of caricatures of celebrities beaming down at them. There's the aptly named "The Little Bar" when you enter, on the left, and upstairs, a copious bar facing a bay of windows that overlook the Broadhurst and Shubert Theaters. It's a place of legendary repute and contains some of its own legends, including the ceremonial applause that greets actors upon their arrival on opening nights.

The ceremonial applause at Sardi's was apparently started back in 1950 when Shirley Booth entered the restaurant to spontaneous acclaim after a career-altering performance in *Come Back, Little Sheba*. The siren song has proven catnip to many, no matter what the circumstances. Actor Lewis J. Stadlen recalls the opening night of *Minnie's Boys* in 1969, when he achieved his own big break playing a young Groucho in the musical biography of the Marx Brothers:

> The producer had planned a big opening night party at Sardi's, but the show had gone through several unexpected weeks of previews and replacements of the creative team. There was no money left, so the opening night party was held in a Chinese restaurant several doors—and a big step—down from Sardi's on 44th Street. But, I thought, the hell with it, I want to go to Sardi's. So, after the Chinese restaurant, my father and I went to Sardi's—and I got an ovation.

Sardi Jr. recounts that "The second round of excitement comes later when the first newspapers arrive.... You can always tell how the box office is going to behave the next day by what happens in Sard's after the reviews come out. If they're good, we start to hear, 'Captain, a bottle of Champagne and the food menu. God, I'm hungry!.' If the reviews aren't good, all we hear is, 'Check, please.'"

On the evening of September 22, 1964, producer Harold Prince decided to hold the opening night party for *Fiddler on the Roof* at the Rainbow Room, sixty floors above Manhattan. Author Richard Altman recounted the sudden change in the atmosphere:

> At 12:15 a.m., word came that Walter Kerr's review in the Herald Tribune was not very good, and minutes later when the Trib was brought in, the high spirits plummeted. Kerr led off by stating: '*Fiddler on the Roof* takes place in Anatevka, a village in Russia, and I think it might be an altogether charming musical if only the people of Anatevka did not pause every now and again to give their regards to Broadway, with remembrances to Herald Square.' Kerr's words wrapped a cloak of melancholy around the Rainbow Room. Jerry Bock and Sheldon [Harnick] left immediately, and, before long, other people began drifting away. The joy was gone; the bubbles had left the Champagne; it seemed best to go home.

Of course, Hal Prince had his ultimate revenge: the show went on to run for eight years on Broadway, despite Kerr's review. Or maybe it was the Champagne itself that got a little high-spirited: at his next opening night, Hal Prince opened a bottle of Champagne in celebration and the cork propelled smack into his chin—he was rushed to the emergency room and required seven stitches.

THE FRENCH '32

(Inspired by *Les Misérables*, 1985)

◇

This Champagne cocktail uses all French ingredients and takes its cue from the popular French '75 cocktail; only in this case, it references the June rebellion of 1832, when a populist battalion of students and citizens took to the streets of Paris to protest the authoritarian rule of King Louis-Phillippe. This event is sketchily limned in during the end of Act One: Gavroche—being the acute political analyst that all ten-year-old boys are—bursts into the tavern to announce that "Lamarque is dead!"—General Lamarque being the leader of the anti-royalist faction. But does it really matter? Drunken students are never a contented lot and all you really need to know is that it's not the French Revolution of 1789 and that it's going to end badly for some of the baritones in the chorus.

CHAMPAGNE
FLUTE

1 La Perruche white sugar cube

¾ ounce crème de cassis (Chambord is high-end, but any will do)

1¼ ounces Cognac

2 ounces French Champagne (don't cut corners here)

Chill a Champagne flute by placing it in the freezer for 5 minutes. Remove and drop in the sugar cube, then build the cocktail by gently adding the cassis, Cognac, and Champagne. Stirring is optional—but if you do, do it gently or you'll get a volcanic eruption in your flute. Me, I like to watch the bubbles float up from the sugar cube on their own.

— DOIN' IT FOR SUGAR —

If you can find them, I strongly suggest using La Perruche sugar cubes rather than more commercial brands. The irregular shape of these cubes is quite attractive in the glass and gives a very nineteenth-century look. And they're French.

THE BABETTE

(Inspired by *On the Twentieth Century*, 1978)

Lily Garland, née Mildred Plotka, is a Golden Age of Hollywood movie star *par excellence*: through her Bel-Air estate, she claims "Champagne's a flowing river." Nice work if you can get it, as Ira Gershwin said.

In *On the Twentieth Century*, Lily finds herself aboard "that luxury of locomotive trains" on a train ride from Chicago to New York, ensconced in the glamourous Art Deco Drawing Room B, while her former lover, down-and-out producer Oscar Jaffee, hidden in Drawing Room A, plots to bring her back to Broadway under his directorial eagle eye. Oscar wants her to play Mary Magdalene in a new stage adaptation. Lily is intrigued—but rival producer Max Jacobs dangles a new Somerset Maugham script with a whacking good part in front of her eyes: "Half brittle, half sardonic, half tragic." "Yes, yes," Lily interjects, "Three halves. Bigger than life!" In the musical number that ensues, Babette is a kept socialite among the "corrupt and debonair" 1920s London Mayfair set that lives for endless loving, boozing, dancing, and cruising. Torn between her two unsatisfying lovers—Rodney and Nigel—she Charlestons the night away, a cocktail in one hand, Champagne in the other, deciding to drown her jitters in gin and bitters. Only a fool would turn down the role, and if anybody is nobody's fool, it's Lily Garland.

CHAMPAGNE
FLUTE

1 ounce Pimm's No. 1 liqueur	2 ounces Champagne or sparkling wine
1 squeeze lemon juice	Lemon peel, for garnish

Chill a Champagne flute by placing it in the freezer for about 5 minutes. Remove and build the cocktail by pouring in the Pimm's first, followed by a squeeze of lemon juice, then the Champagne. Stir gently. Garnish with a lemon peel.

Lily and Oscar take a sixteen-hour train ride aboard the Twentieth Century Limited. I wouldn't advise more than one Babette every four hours. . .

LA PASSEGGIATA

(Inspired by *The Light in the Piazza*, 2003)

In the musical version of *The Light in the Piazza*, nearly half the scenes take place in the multiple public squares (piazzas) in Florence (and one in Rome). Even the most casual observer would notice the various outdoor tables at cafés, where tourists and natives alike take a break to enjoy an espresso or even a spritz, an afternoon cocktail of unsurpassed refreshment. Despite even the mild alcoholic content of such a beverage, it's unlikely that the peremptory maternal instinct of Margaret Johnson would allow her daughter, Clara, to order a spritz—and she probably wouldn't even order one for herself, given her Southern propriety.

Still, it's the perfect drink to enjoy before or after a *passeggiata*—a languid stroll through the city and the title of yet another rhapsodic melody by Adam Guettel from the musical—or while listening to a *passacaglia,* a romantic tune that takes "strolling" as part of its name.

This cocktail uses prosecco, the more casual sparkling white wine of Italy, and changes it up a bit from the Aperol spritz now found nearly ubiquitously, thanks to the heavy promotion of the clever owners of Aperol liqueur. It employs, instead, a particularly light and floral version of Ramazzotti, another venerated Italian liqueur, which seems fitting for this musical.

COUPE

1 ounce Cointreau or triple sec
1 ounce Ramazzotti Aperitivo Rosato (orange blossom and hibiscus)

2 ounces prosecco
Soda, if using
1 orange slice, for garnish

Fill a Champagne coupe (not a flute) with ice. Add the Cointreau
or triple sec and Ramazzotti, then the prosecco. Top with soda water,
if you like, and garnish with the orange slice.
Enjoy the setting rays of the Tuscan sun, as they gild the statues
in the square. If a lady's hat should flutter by in the wind,
it's your call if you want to get up and chase it.

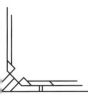

CHAPTER 2

Prohibition

SYNCOPATED
COCKTAIL

———————————◇———————————

Now that your drinking days are through,
Come along with me;
I've got a brand-new jag for you—
It's a melody.
Syncopated music
Goes right to your head . . .
Come along and have
A syncopated cocktail with me.
—Irving Berlin (1919)

During the years 1919 to 1933—the bookends of Prohibition—Broadway was like a chorus girl in one of the many revues that prospered during the Twenties: changing costumes constantly, but still frequently recognizable and always entertaining.

By the time the 1920s began, Broadway had evolved into the legendary institution that has been an essential element in American culture for more than a century. The Theater District had become a locus for entertainment around Times Square. Dozens of theaters sprang up, and the newly created subway was the virtual circulatory system that brought tourists and audiences streaming in and out of the West Forties. A robust nightlife supported the theatrical productions of Broadway; given that the diurnal rhythms of the neighborhood came to life after the curtain came down, restaurants, bars, and night clubs operated into the wee small hours. In artfully curated and expansive eating establishments such as Rector's or Sherry's, elegant parqueted floors held dozens of tables under vaulted ceilings, while the waiters served Lobster Thermidor, oysters on the half shell, and Baked Alaska. The Champagne flowed, rare Alsatian wines were uncorked, and celebrities toasted their latest triumphs with glistening tankards of foaming ale. No respectable establishment was without a small salon orchestra and, toward the end of the 1910s, enterprising restauranteurs removed many of their best tables to create an intimate dance floor in the middle of the dining room for adventuresome couples who wanted to test out the Grizzly Bear or the Fox Trot. The dozens of eating and drinking emporia that twinkled like sequins along the beaded gown of Times Square were a glowing testament to the burgeoning consumerism of an emerging nation—it was a public demonstration of celebrity, degustation, intoxication, and laughter.

And it all came to a screeching halt on January 19, 1920.

WHO'S THAT DAPPER, HAPPY-GO-LUCKY SON OF BROADWAY?

Prohibition of the manufacture, sale, or transportation of alcoholic beverages—or more accurately, the Eighteenth Amendment to the Constitution—had been bruited about by temperance organizations across the nation for decades. It did not creep upon the denizens of Broadway "softly as in a morning sunrise," as Oscar Hammerstein II's lyric in 1926's *The Desert Song* would have it. The *Ziegfeld Follies of 1919* prefigured this catastrophe with several songs about the incipient removal of one of America's favorite pastimes: Eddie Cantor reminded audiences in the New Amsterdam that "You Don't Need the Wine to Have a Wonderful Time" and Bert Williams bemoaned the circumstances "When the Moon Shines on the Moonshine." Irving Berlin composed a production number for show girls costumed as Sarsaparilla and Coca-Cola—the kind of denatured effervescence cosmopolitan Manhattanites were now expected to endure—in a production number called "Syncopated Cocktail."

PREVIOUS SPREAD
I don't mean rhinestones: Megan Hilty and Rachel York celebrate a holiday from Prohibition while gold-digging in Europe in an Encores! concert version of *Gentlemen Prefer Blondes* (2012).

ABOVE The raffish figure of Mayor James J. Walker inspired several musical numbers and one entire musical: *Jimmy* (1969) starring Frank Gorshin as "Gentleman Jimmy." It lasted shorter than all of Walker's 1927 vacation days put together.

As the year 1920 lumbered along, New Yorkers were in a heck of a spot. The Volstead Act, a concurrent piece of Congressional legislation, left the direct implementation of the Eighteenth Amendment to the respective states; each would decide how and when the law would be enforced. Luckily for those who preferred a good time, the mayor of New York City was a former songwriter, bon vivant, and scoundrel who "looked the other way" so often from the onerous obligations of enforcement that he should have been prescribed a neck brace. Mayor James J. Walker was once profiled by the *New York Daily News*: "Whatever his critics may say about him, the glib, wise-cracking and debonair Jimmy made himself a national institution. The Walker administration will go down in the annals as a good-time-Charlie, whoop-de-do, never-to-be-forgotten three-ring circus."

Walker was, perhaps, the most theatrical figure New Yorkers had ever known—he certainly appeared as a character in more musicals than any other historical figure of the time. In the *Ziegfeld Follies of 1927*, he was spoofed by Eddie Cantor in a Berlin song entitled "My New York": "And what chance a Jones? / With the Cohns and Malones / in my New York?" He made a cameo—via a campaign rally—in *Fiorello!* (1958), apostrophized in a song called "Gentleman Jimmy." And he was finally given his own (short-lived) musical, *Jimmy*, starring Frank Gorshin, where his swagger and philandering were given center stage. A married Catholic, Walker had a

LEFT Director Billy Wilder turned the gangland St. Valentine's Day massacre of 1929 into his hilarious film *Some Like It Hot*, which in turn became a 1972 musical, *Sugar*. Tony Roberts (left) and the beloved Robert Morse provide the laughs in drag.

mistress, Betty Compton, who was a Broadway show girl—and, of course, she was given plenty of 1920s pastiche numbers in the musical.

The fact that Walker himself oversaw the 1929 renovation of a Central Park nightclub called the Casino as a showplace for his cronies and other celebrities didn't exactly burnish his reputation for civic rectitude. (He did hire Joseph Urban, Ziegfeld's favorite designer, to do the interiors.) Walker's frequent *volte-faces* regarding the enforcement of Prohibition transformed the city's atmosphere from its post-Victorian exuberance to a grittier, more clandestine, and furtive one. The new nightspot during Prohibition was the speakeasy—an unmarked, unadvertised club or series of rooms where all kinds of liquor could be served without the refinements of dance floors, mahogany bars, or even menus. The booze itself was unrefined, unremarkable, and cheap—at least cheap to produce; the mark-up for the stuff was astronomical. No one seemed to mind; the number of speakeasies that opened (and shuttered) in New York City during Prohibition is impossible to ascertain, given that their anonymity precluded an official tally. but estimates varied from 32,000 to 100,000.

Some speakeasies were low-key—what we would call "under the radar"—and the very secretive and transitory aspect of the speakeasy was part of its charm. To evade the rare police raid, the 21 Club had a special chute built that would send the evening's entire quota of liquor conveniently down to the cellar, where the bottles would be smashed mechanically, thereby eliminating the evidence. Other speakeasies were more overt, more like nightclubs that flaunted their existence in front of the jaded and wearied eye of law enforcement. Still, patrons at the El Fey Club or the Hotsy Totsy or the Silver Slipper knew they were getting a higher grade of illegal alcohol for their hard-earned dollars, thanks to the clubs' connection with organized crime. Bootleggers and gangsters formed the last

corner of the Prohibition triangle—along with speakeasies and jazz—and their influence on the nightlife of Broadway in the 1920s, both in reality and in legend, was formidable indeed.

If Prohibition was meant to curb the disagreeable side of human behavior, it certainly failed where criminality was concerned; the full blossom of organized crime in America was cultivated, as it were, by the irrigation. of illegal hooch. Consumers wanted alcohol, and here was a clever and resourceful counter-industry ready to fill that need through methods that were tried and not necessarily true. The illegal transportation of alcohol was managed in many places across the country, but the coast of Long Island (only a few hours' motorboat ride to Manhattan's docks) were particularly conducive to bootlegging and rumrunning. The ease with which organized criminals could provide liquor to a thirsty, but law-abiding, public made them the object of gratitude, rather than approbation, and celebrity inevitably followed. Gangsters in New York, such as Owney Madden and Connie Immerman, ran and operated successful nightclubs where their entrepreneurship and presence were publicly celebrated.

I FOLLOW WINCHELL AND READ EV'RY LINE

Recognizable, glamorous, and dangerous, the Prohibition-era gangster became fodder for popular culture in newspapers, magazines, silent (and, soon, talking) pictures, and Broadway musicals. As early as 1926, the Gershwins' *Oh, Kay!* framed its romantic plot with a story of rumrunners evading the law while hiding out in a Long Island mansion. The framework of that musical "inspired" the 2012 show *Nice Work if You Can Get It*, which was cobbled together out of a random selection of Gershwin tunes into a story about bootleggers and playboys. Other shows featuring musically minded Prohibition gangsters include *Sugar*, an adaptation of *Some Like It Hot*, where gangleader Spats Columbo executes

his rivals by tap-dancing them to death; Woody Allen's *Bullets Over Broadway*; *Legs Diamond*, an infamous bomb starring Peter Allen; and *Windy City*, a West End musical based on *The Front Page*, the 1928 classic play that already contained a gangster or two. (One could probably include *Funny Girl*, given that its romantic leading man, gambler Nicky Arnstein, went to prison a couple of times for embezzlement—in real life, anyway.) Perhaps the most curious of these was the 1962 flop *Nowhere to Go But Up*, based on the real-life exploits of Izzy Einstein and Moe Smith, federal agents who adopted a whole range of disguises and got up to all sorts of shenanigans to protect Prohibition regulations. The lyrics were by James Lipton—later known for hosting *Inside the Actors Studio*—and the show's director was Sidney

Lumet, one of the twentieth century's great film directors, but all thumbs when it came to musicals. *Nowhere to Go But Up* went down after a week of performances.

Gangsters weren't the only celebrities created out of the raucous cacophony of Prohibition. The most famous of these held court at Larry Fay's El Fey Club: the peerless compere Texas Guinan, a former vaudevillian who flaunted her minimal talent and maximal personality to the free-spending customers with the legendary phrase "Hello, suckers!" Guinan was such a vibrant mascot for flouting the rules of Prohibition that after a series of Broadway shows (including Mae West's comedy *Sex*) were briefly padlocked by a law-abiding police commissioner (Jimmy Walker had taken a vacation out of town), she opened her

ABOVE Producer Earl Carroll was famous for saying that through the stage door of his theater passed "the most beautiful girls in the world." Here he is with a few of them backstage,

own Broadway musical revue called *The Padlocks of 1927*. One of Guinan's most frequent customers was gossip columnist Walter Winchell, who practically created the mythical world of Broadway hip-hooray and ballyhoo in his *Daily Mirror* column (and, later, radio program). For Winchell, a former vaudeville hoofer, the elegant stars of Broadway were indistinguishable from its colorful riff-raff; anyone who did anything worthy of an item in his column—getting a standing ovation, getting a divorce, getting drunk, getting shot—was a celebrity. Broadway honored him in its own way, featuring fictional versions of his vulpine vindictiveness in such musicals as *Animal Crackers*, *It's a Bird... It's a Plane... It's SUPERMAN!*, and *Sweet Smell of Success*.

IN SOME SECLUDED RENDEZVOUS

One of the characters to whom Winchell gave a lot of ink was producer Earl Carroll, perhaps the epitome of the showbiz razzle-dazzle of the Prohibition age. Carroll was a mediocre songwriter who parlayed his instinct for publicity into a robust career as a revue producer on Broadway beginning in 1923 and lasting into the

1930s. Knowing full well that Florenz Ziegfeld had the resources to present the most expensive comedians and the most gorgeous setting in his *Follies*, Carroll pivoted to shine the spotlight on the one thing Prohibition-era audiences seemed to want most (after decent booze): girls, preferably in the flimsiest state on habiliment. His *Earl Carroll Vanities* publicly claimed to hire his chorines from the ranks of local beauty contest winners—although he just as frequently failed to make good on his promises of a featured role in the chorus. In an era that respected the latest catch phrase, the motto that adorned the entrance to the stage door of his eponymous theater was among the most widely quoted: "Through These Portals Pass the Most Beautiful Girls in the World."

Carroll's chief goal in life was getting his name into the city's more than one dozen local daily newspapers; in February of 1926, his grasp exceeded his reach. As a ritual, on every Washington's birthday, Carroll held a massive after-hours party on the stage of his theater for his pals and investors. On this occasion, stagehands pushed out a bathtub on wheels,

popped open what were ostensibly Champagne bottles and poured them into the bathtub, whereupon an out-of-work chorus girl named Joyce Hawley scurried across the stage in a green overcoat, doffed it quickly and dove in the tub, covered by nothing but bubbles. A line of patrons queued up and dipped their glasses into the, um, intoxicating brew. Carroll apparently hoped that news of his party would be kept on the down-low; in that case, he shouldn't have invited the editor of the *Daily Mirror*.

Within three months, Carroll was hauled into federal court—not for bringing out a nude woman in public (although he had been arrested for a lobby display featuring nude chorus girls a few years earlier)—but for bringing out a bathtub full of Champagne. On the stand, Carroll claimed the bubbly bathwater only *looked* like Champagne. The jury didn't believe him and he was convicted of perjury. The *New Yorker*, which covered the trial, wrote: "It is likely that some enterprising daily paper will contract with him for a daily dispatch on prison life. And that will be more valuable as publicity than half-a-dozen chorus girl parades on Broadway. Already I envision the headline: 'Carroll Directs Vanities Show from Prison Cell.'" Carroll wound up serving six months in jail, making him the only Prohibition-era Broadway celebrity to serve time (other than Mae West, who spent eight days in prison on Welfare Island in 1927 on obscenity charges for her Broadway production of *Sex*). When talkies came along, Carroll segued into movies. One of them, *Murder at the Vanities*, continued his combined interest in booze and showbiz by introducing the song "Cocktails for Two."

HARLEM—IN ERMINE AND PEARLS

Carroll realized, like many motivated characters in the 1920s, that there was no such thing as bad publicity. A neophyte reporter for the *Chicago Tribune* named Maurine Watkins realized the

RIGHT The star role of Reno Sweeney in *Anything Goes* was fashioned for Ethel Merman in the original 1934 production, but the larger-than-life character—a kind of mash-up of Texas Guinan and Aimee Semple McPherson— was subsequently played in various revivals by Patti LuPone and Elaine Paige (seen here in the London 1989 version).

OPPOSITE Carol Channing was not the first (nor the last) actor to embody the carefree acquisitiveness of Anita Loos's Lorelei Lee, but she was the most legendary. Here is she is, plotting her destiny with gal-pal Dorothy Shaw (Yvonne Adair) from the 1949 Broadway production.

veracity of that statement when she profiled four murderesses lined up in cells along Cook County Prison's Death Row in 1924. You couldn't make up such real-life characters as the killers Watkins profiled, but a few years later, she decided that she might as well make up some more. Her embroidered account, now fictionalized as a Broadway play, brought *Chicago* to New York and acquainted audiences with an unsentimental murderess named Roxie Hart. After two movie versions, Watkins's courtroom potboiler was adapted by Bob Fosse, John Kander, and Fred Ebb in 1975 as a musical—which added the extra appeal of evanescent fame in vaudeville. Eventually, *Chicago* became an international phenomenon, underscored by fantastic music and lyrics and set apart by cold gin and a hot piano.

Fred Ebb's trenchant lyrics to the opening number of *Chicago* refer, of course, to jazz—"all that jazz"—and the opening number features a throw to a trumpeter named "Father Dip": an inaccurate, but endearing neologism that references Louis Armstrong, known as "Pops" or "Dippermouth." By the late 1920s, Armstrong himself had moved from Chicago, where things were hot enough to boil over, to Harlem, New York, which was the epicenter of Black culture in America, and the world. There, the many jazz nightclubs kept the rhythm of the cutting-edge culture; places such as Connie's Inn, Minton's, Small's Paradise, and the Cotton Club were the hot spots, percolators of such immense talents as Ethel Waters—who was a soul singer before the term was invented—Lena Horne, Cab Calloway, John Bubbles, and many other Black entertainers who made the journey downtown to Broadway, where they broke barriers and expanded their influence on American culture. Armstrong himself sojourned briefly on Broadway in 1929

RIGHT Run by gangsters, attended by white audiences, but made famous by some of the finest Black talent that America has ever known, Connie's Inn in Harlem was one of New York's most revered nightclubs during the Prohibition years.

when *Hot Chocolates*, a revue that began at Connie's Inn—owned by the white gangster Connie Immerman—moved downtown to the Hudson Theater. One of the revue's highlights was when Armstrong blasted the "Fats" Waller/ Andy Razaf tune "Ain't Misbehavin'" from the orchestra pit. Audiences were so enthralled by his virtuosity that they demanded he play and sing his solo from the stage and, so, Satchmo—not the first and certainly not the last explosive Black personality from the Jazz Age to get a Broadway spotlight—made his theatrical debut.

THE WORLD'S GONE MAD TODAY

Halfway through the Broadway run of *Hot Chocolates*, the Stock Market crashed, bringing the freewheeling antics of the Twenties to an exhausted closing number. Prohibition continued as an ever-weakening curtain call for another three years, brought to an exit only when Franklin D. Roosevelt took office. By the end of his first year and the adoption of the Twenty-first Amendment in December of 1933, Repeal became official.

Times Square changed nearly overnight. The covert, illicit, tantalizing chorus girl of Prohibition shed her flimsy flapper garments for something more reasonable and—despite Repeal—sober. Alcohol was back, but now it was publicly acceptable and of higher quality. Restauranteurs and entrepreneurs realized that consumers no longer wanted to drink in the shadows, nor did they want to get clipped by drinking inferior rotgut at exorbitant prices. A new kind of establishment emerged in the Theater District in the 1930s: the supper club, a version of the nightclub without the speakeasy connotation. The epitome of this trend was Billy Rose's Diamond Horseshoe on West 46th Street. Rose, a producer and songwriter (and the third husband of Fanny Brice) created an emporium that offered first-class entertainment, a full orchestra, white-jacketed waiters serving chicken pot pie and lamb chops, prefaced by old-fashioneds and Planter's Punch at reasonable prices, on tables with white linen tablecloths. The menu listed more than forty cocktails. It was the kind of place immortalized in countless RKO movies during the Depression and brought an elegant respectability back to Broadway nightlife.

After the excrescences of Prohibition, respectability and elegance were key to Broadway's identity, even with the deprivations of the Depression. Perhaps no musical summed up this transition better than Cole Porter's *Anything Goes*. Initially assembled during the height of Prohibition in 1930, it was delayed three years because the show's setting—an ocean liner—was considered inappropriate after an actual luxury liner caught fire off the New Jersey coast, killing scores of passengers. *Anything Goes* invites some of the Prohibition era's most venerable tropes up the gangplank for one last voyage: there's a gangster, a nightclub hostess, contraband cargo, and, of course, anything set on a ship reminded audiences of rumrunning and bootlegging. Porter himself missed most of Prohibition—he spent the 1920s in Europe, drinking Champagne and Sidecars in Paris and Venice, but surely the sentiments of the song "Anything Goes"—"the world's gone mad today"—summed up the headier days of the Roaring Twenties.

As suggested by *Anything Goes*, Broadway had a hard time letting go of the Prohibition era. In fact, probably more than any other era, the Twenties have been reprised in dozens of subsequent musicals over the decades. There have been showbiz sagas (*Gypsy, Funny Girl, Sophie, Minnie's Boys, Mack & Mabel, Chaplin*); pastiches (*Billion Dollar Baby, The Boy Friend, The Drowsy Chaperone*); revivals (*No, No, Nanette, Good News, Oh, Kay!*); adaptations of original 1920s material (*My One and Only, Nice Work If You Can Get It, Bullets Over Broadway*); adaptations of material set in the 1920s (*Sugar, Chicago, Singin' in the*

Rain, *Victor/Victoria, The Wild Party, By Jeeves, Thoroughly Modern Millie*); and tributes to the Black experience of the decade (*Bubbling Brown Sugar, Eubie!, Sophisticated Ladies, Jelly's Last Jam, After Midnight, Shuffle Along*).

One essential piece of Twenties source material received two separate bites of the Broadway musical apple: Anita Loos's 1925 novella, *Gentlemen Prefer Blondes,* about the eternally optimistic and resourceful Lorelei Lee, who is the quintessential Jazz Age flapper. Adapted for the musical stage first in 1949—making a star out of Carol Channing—the story followed Lorelei across the sea on an ocean liner (shades of *Anything Goes*) and chronicled her attempts to land the right kind of sugar daddy in Europe. It was subsequently adapted for the movies—making a legend out of Marilyn Monroe—and revised for a 1974 version called *Lorelei,* where Channing once again inhabited the role, this time with a flashback frame and the inclusion of some additional songs.

Clearly, the appeal of Prohibition-era shenanigans had a long throw. It must be the tap-dancing, the illegality, the costumes, the celebrity culture, the urban excitement, the carefree disregard for conventional morality, the bathtub gin. . . .

Oh, and all that jazz.

LEFT Billy Rose—impresario, lyricist, and husband of Fanny Brice—reinvented the New York nightclub scene, post-Prohibition, with the Diamond Horseshoe.

THE HOT HONEY FLIP

(Inspired by *Chicago*, 1975)

When Bob Fosse constructed his *chef d'oeuvre, Chicago,* he combined several ingredients that he knew and understood by heart: showbiz, vaudeville, exploitation—*some* of the things that we hold near and dear to our hearts.

One thing that was pretty much left out of a show about Chicago, however, was booze. Illegal booze certainly primed the pump of the actual Chicago in the 1920s; the entire edifice of organized crime in the Midwest was built on the stuff. Canada had a much spottier Prohibition movement in the 1920s, and so Canadian distillers such as Seagram's made a fortune shipping their whiskeys along Lake Michigan, so that they might be unloaded secretly in the Windy City.

The Hot Honey Flip takes its inspiration from a stiff pour of whiskey, as a nod to our Canadian friends, as well as a delightfully diverting product found at gourmet markets called hot honey, which is exactly what it sounds like: honey with a cayenne kick.

Speaking of kicks, the "Hot Honey Rag" is the concluding dance number in *Chicago.* It follows "Nowadays," but was left off the original Broadway Cast album. Fosse experimented on the road with an ending that would showcase the "merry murderesses" Roxie Hart and Velma Kelly and their big break as a vaudeville act. His first couple of passes emphasized the fact that they—that is, the characters—weren't very talented as vaudevillians, but no one in the Philadelphia tryout audience believed (or wanted to believe) for a second that Gwen Verdon and Chita Rivera, who played the parts, weren't capable of bringing down the house. So, Fosse caved to the public's preferences and choreographed one of the classic duets in Broadway history.

LOWBALL

1 or 2 tablespoons hot honey, to taste

2 ounces bourbon or whiskey

1 ounce Seagram's 7 Crown dark honey whiskey

Crushed ice

Pour the hot honey into a lowball glass, then add the whiskeys.
Stir vigorously at first, and then add the ice at the end—otherwise,
the ice will harden the honey and make it difficult to blend.

THE GLIMPSE OF STOCKING

(Inspired by *Anything Goes*, 1934)

Cole Porter always knew how to live the high life; in fact, he set the bar—especially when it came to bars. Porter also knew that when it came to the blues, there was "no cure like travel," as the opening number of *Anything Goes* puts it. The songwriter was always inspired by a sojourn on an ocean liner—where other collaborators might bang out their latest musical in a stuffy office in the West Forties, Porter took Moss Hart, his book writer for the 1935 musical Jubilee, on a five-month worldwide cruise on the S.S. Franconia instead.

Anything Goes hints at the top shelf nature of Porter's tastes when it comes to alcohol. In "You're the Top," the leading characters compare each other to Napoleon brandy and a Ritz (as in the hotel) hot toddy. And the same characters get such a kick out of each other that, by comparison, Champagne and "mere alcohol" doesn't thrill them at all.

This particular cocktail might not be looked on as something shocking, exactly, but it's based on a gin-based drink called the Tuxedo, which dates back before the nineteenth century. Of course, Porter always looked exquisite in a tuxedo and, knowing the dress codes of a luxury liner as well as he did, he surely would have sported one while dining at the captain's table. The look of this drink is supposed to conjure up the sun setting on the blue horizon, glimpsed over the quarterdeck railing. It's Pepsodent!

MARTINI
+ COCTAIL SHAKER

- **1 or 2 spritzes absinthe**
- **2 ounces clear gin, preferably Plymouth Gin (as in Plymouth Rock)**
- **1 ounce dry vermouth**
- **1 ounce maraschino liqueur, such as Luxardo**
- **1 dash blue curacao syrup**
- **1 circular lemon wheel, to garnish**

Chill a martini glass by putting it in the freezer for about 5 minutes. When chilled, spray two spritzes of absinthe in the glass. In a shaker, add ice and pour the remaining ingredients, except the lemon, over the ice. Shake and strain the contents into the martini glass. Slice the lemon halfway through the diameter and set it on the glass's rim so that it looks like a setting sun in the turquoise light of a summer night in Spain.

THE LORELEI

(Inspired by *Gentlemen Prefer Blondes*, 1949)

The Lorelei is a conceit of German folklore, based on a misty maiden who, perched on a rock in the middle of the Rhine, enthralled passing sailors and drove them to their doom.

Lorelei Lee, the heroine of Anita Loos's 1925 novella *Gentlemen Prefer Blondes*, was enamored of a different kind of rock: one of the 1.75 carat variety. As a morally centered but ethically challenged flapper of the Jazz Age, Lorelei had her priorities straight: "A kiss on the hand may make you feel very nice, but a diamond and sapphire bracelet lasts forever." When she travels with her gal pal, Dorothy Shaw, to Europe on the *Ile de France*, she not only bypasses the un-wet blanket of Prohibition, she also avails herself of numerous opportunities to encounter the potential sugar daddies who can underwrite her carefree existence.

Loos's book was an instant success, and Lorelei, along with Jay Gatsby and Mickey Mouse, became one of the most enduring characters of the 1920s. She appeared in a Broadway play, a comic strip, and, in 1949, a Broadway musical that will forever link her character to Carol Channing.

This cocktail waves its bracelet in the direction of Lorelei's trip to France. It uses French vermouth and Canton liqueur (French-based, despite the *chinoiserie* in the name)—with a little bit of Italy. What's really important about this cocktail is that it be given the sparkle of diamonds, which are not only forever, but also a girl's best friend. (And after you reach for the cocktail shaker, make sure you get that ice—or else, no dice!)

ROCKS
+ COCTAIL SHAKER

1 ounce dry vermouth
1 ounce grappa
1 ounce Canton ginger liqueur
Rock-candy swizzle stick

Add the vermouth, grappa, and Canton liqueur to a cocktail shaker and shake. Pour the mixture into a rocks glass and stir three times with the rock-candy swizzle stick. Set the swizzle stick aside for later; you don't want the drink to be too sweet.

CHAPTER 3

Luminaries

INTEMPERATE
TOTS

The night sky of Broadway is studded with constellations of drinkers and folks who wrote about drinking (often, but not always, the same person), but within those galaxies there were a few luminaries who shone the way with their unique star quality. Among them were two playwrights, one songwriter, one actor—and one celebrity who was all three.

Any playwright worth his or her salty pretzel knows how to set a scene in a bar or how to summon up a fractious confrontation between two inebriates (or even four inebriates: see Edward Albee's *Who's Afraid of Virginia Woolf?*). Eugene O'Neill could do them one step better; he could even render the rundown bar in his *The Iceman Cometh* with as much—if not more—character description than some of the characters. Harry Hope's joint was, in O'Neill's stage directions, "a cheap Ginmill of the five-cent whiskey, last-resort variety." The bar nominally follows the rules of "Raines-Law," a municipal ordinance that allowed bars to stay open on Sundays, as long as they serve something resembling food, which meant "putting a property sandwich in the middle of each table, an old desiccated ruin of dust-laden bread and mummified ham or cheese which only the drunkest yokel from the sticks ever regarded as anything but a noisome table decoration."

Tennessee Williams—certainly O'Neill's heir apparent in rendering the mythology of American alcoholism—was capable of apostrophizing liquor into something akin to how the poets of the Elizabethan age rendered homage unto their queen. In "Notes to the Director," written as a preface for *Cat on a Hot Tin Roof*, Williams uses his poetic talent to create one of literature's only odes to a liquor cabinet—and surely its most elegant:

> **(On stage) there is a monumental monstrosity peculiar to our times, a huge console combination of radio-phonograph (Hi-Fi with three speakers), TV set, and liquor cabinet, bearing and containing many glasses and bottles, all in one piece, which is a composition of muted silver tones, and the opalescent tones of reflecting glass, a chromatic link, this thing, between the sepia (tawny gold) tones of the interior and the cool (white and blue) tones of the gallery and sky. This piece of furniture (?!), this monument, is a very complete and compact little shrine to virtually all the comforts and Illusions behind which we hide from such things as the characters in the play are faced with.**

That's the work of someone who knows their way around a liquor cabinet. So, to this luminary—and his colleagues, most of whom Williams had shared a bar stool with at one time or another—let's propose a toast.

PREVIOUS SPREAD Harry Hope's bar—aka "The No Chance Saloon, The End of the Line Café"—from Eugene O'Neill's immortal *The Iceman Cometh*, here seen in the 1999 revival.

EUGENE O'NEILL

"Gimme a whiskey—ginger ale on the side. And don't be stingy, baby."
—*Anna Christie*

It's not terribly surprising that, in addition to being America's first great playwright, Eugene O'Neill should provide us with the first cocktail recipe in modern drama, courtesy of Anna Christie's opening line.

O'Neill's play, *Anna Christie*, which premiered on Broadway in 1921 (and won the second of his four Pulitzer Prizes) is characteristically set in a saloon, a waterfront dive called Jimmy-the-Priest's on the West Side of Lower Manhattan. Nearly all of O'Neill's major plays—*Anna Christie, A Touch of the Poet, Ah, Wilderness!, The Iceman Cometh*—have some scene or another that takes place in a tavern or saloon, and those that aren't specifically set in dives—*The Hairy Ape, Long Day's Journey Into Night, A Moon for the Misbegotten*—feature some deep dive into the universe of drinkers and their private versions of hell.

O'Neill came to his braiding of theater and alcohol honestly. He was born in 1888 in a hotel room on Broadway and the West Forties, decades before the area became the glamorous Theater District. His father, James O'Neill, was a touring actor of some repute—if not superstardom—who had bought the lucrative rights to a stage version of *The Count of Monte Cristo*. The elder O'Neill, when the box office receipts turned a profit, was known to be a convivial toast-raiser in whatever bars adjoined the theaters on tour, although, apparently, he was more at home with

the cocktail *du jour*—a gin rickey, say—than a pint of lager or a shot of rot gut.

Throughout his post-adolescent days, young Eugene was not quite so exacting. From his late teens to the end of World War I, O'Neill's life seems to have been one long bender, with him drowning his sorrows (and insecurities) at

ABOVE Eugene O'Neill as captured by legendary photographer Carl Van Vechten.

barrooms and brothels in Hell's Kitchen, the Tenderloin, and Greenwich Village, often in the company of his elder brother Jamie, who would eventually die of acute alcoholism. On the few times he came up for air, O'Neill traveled by merchant ship south of the border or wrote short plays or both; needless to say, perhaps, the ministrations of alcohol helped him get through his turbulent twenties and thirties, although his choice of liquor seemed to be whatever was near at hand—vile stuff, often flirting with toxicity.

By 1926, having attained commercial and critical success on Broadway (as well as two Pulitzers and a handful of film adaptations), O'Neill apparently put his hard drinking behind him for the rest of his life—although he would occasionally be bumped off the wagon by some familial complication or a bad production. From the mid-1920s to the end of World War II, he enjoyed the status of the most honored and respected playwright of the American stage. Whatever personal demons he had to exorcise to transform his imagination into dialogue and stage settings, as well as the physical obstacles he overcame—he suffered neurological and physiological ailments one wouldn't wish on their worst enemy, let alone America's greatest playwright—O'Neill's name on a theater marquee assured audiences of integrity and high-mindedness, however bizarre or ambitious his most recent enterprise might be.

According to his own account, O'Neill was personally disciplined when it came to that thin line between inspiration and inebriation: "The artist drinks, when he drinks at all, for relaxation, forgetfulness, excitement, for any purpose except his art. You've got to have all your critical and creative faculties about you when you're working. I never try to write a line when I'm not strictly on the wagon."

Such critical distance allowed O'Neill to create substantial compassion for the deluded inebriated souls who populate his oeuvre. His early years as a barfly taught O'Neill "not to sit in judgment of other people." Perhaps even more so than for his characters, the playwright showed compassion (and a fine sense of detail) for the backroom haunts of his past and he immortalized several of his earlier training grounds in his 1939 (but not performed until 1946) opus, *The Iceman Cometh*.

The play takes place in 1912 in Harry Hope's bar, an amalgam of Jimmy-the-Priest's at 252 Fulton Street and the Golden Swan, a bar that catered to Greenwich Village customers in the shadow of the elevated tracks at Sixth Avenue and West 4th Street.

But beyond its apposite location, Hope's bar has a larger existential implication. One of its bartenders describes it thus: "What is it? It's the No Chance Saloon. It's Bedrock Bar, The End of the Line Cafe, The Bottom of the Sea Rathskeller. It's the last harbor. No one here has to worry about where they're going next, because there's no farther they can go. It's a great comfort to them." The play's leading character, Theodore "Hickey" Hickman, comes by once a year and buys several rounds for the dissipated regulars because "he never runs into anyone he knows in his business here." But, as the regulars point out, during one of Hickey's more garrulous displays, "All we want is to pass out and get drunk and a little peace."

Iceman took a while to catch on—its original Broadway production left some head-scratching in its wake, but a 1956 Off-Broadway revival starring Jason Robards Jr. in a part he was destined to play (indeed, he assayed Hickey twice more) restored the play to its high shelf in American drama (it would reappear on Broadway four more times). Whatever its *longeurs* and flaws, *The Iceman Cometh* certainly is the American saloon play *par excellence*; anyone attempting to set their play in a bar or saloon subsequently does so knowingly in the long shadow thrown by O'Neill's masterpiece.

Eugene O'Neill may have seen life through a shot glass darkly, but no playwright ever did so in a more illuminating and—dare one say?—sobering way.

LEFT O'Neill's only comedy—a relative term—*Ah, Wilderness!*—was turned into the jolly 1958 musical *Take Me Along* that gave Jackie Gleason a star turn as the recidivist boozehound Uncle Sid. Gleason brought, shall we say, experience to the role and won a Tony Award.

NOËL COWARD

Cocktails and laughter,
But what comes after?
Nobody knows.
—**"Poor Little Rich Girl"**

To be an accomplished actor in the plays of Noël Coward, one needs to master three important skills: how to process and articulate sophisticated thoughts at the speed of light; how to know your lines without bumping into the furniture (Coward's own dictum); and how to mix a drink and serve it with impeccable charm.

Noël Coward was one of the most impressive figures ever to bestride the theatrical stage. Born two weeks before the twentieth century, the British writer-director-songwriter-star-you-name-it became a national celebrity at the age of 24 and, within a few years, conquered Broadway and eventually, by the early 1930s, the world at large. That's not to say that Coward didn't have his ups and downs. He was considered somewhat passé by the angry young men of the British Theatre in the Fifties; and the Sixties produced a profound change in musical theater that seemed completely out of step with his witty sentimentality. But Coward had, as he usually did, the last laugh. He was knighted in 1970, won an honorary Tony Award in 1971 for lifetime achievement, and passed away peacefully at his enchanting Jamaican estate in 1973.

Posterity—or its lazy cousin—has handed down a stereotypical image of Coward wrapped in a Sulka dressing gown with a cigarette holder in one hand and a martini waving about in the other. Although the cigarette was an omnipresent accessory, drinks rarely were. Coward's own relation to alcohol was most often judicious, occasionally celebratory, but never self-damaging. Throughout his career, which lasted half a century, and produced dozens of plays,

musicals, screenplays, and hundreds of songs, Coward typically woke up around six in the morning and was at the typewriter by seven. When a civilized lunchtime arrived, he would pull the last dozen or so pages out of the typewriter, put them in a box, and graciously retire somewhere elegant for lunch, perhaps accompanied by the lubricating reward of a martini.

"Made a vow to give up drinking," he once wrote in his diary. "I don't need it. I don't particularly like it, it makes me feel dull and heavy... it is fattening and boring, and so no more of it." That sounds about right, although the diary entry three weeks later refers to "too many martinis" at lunch—mind you, that day Coward was having lunch with the head of British Intelligence. The charting of Coward's drinking would be dreadfully dull compared to, say, that of O'Neill or Tennessee Williams, except for the fact that when he drinks socially, he does so at the most interesting places with the most interesting people. His diaries refer to a roundelay of backstage drinks after a performance with Marlene or Vivien and Larry, say, or cocktail parties for the luminaries of stage, screen, and the known world—including Winston Churchill and the Duke of Windsor. A round of cocktails while the sun was setting in his various homes in Bermuda, Jamaica, and Switzerland are cast as the crowning touch to a hard day's work, either at the typewriter or on the rehearsal stage or both.

Where Coward and alcohol intersect most beautifully and appropriately are in various scenes from his Immortal plays. Simply put, there is

RIGHT In his mid-fifties, Noël Coward surprised everyone—except himself perhaps—by becoming a cabaret star at a Las Vegas hotel. In a photo shoot staged in the Nevada desert, Coward maintains his legendary sangfroid. Cheers!

hardly a major play of Coward's that does not contain some sort of event where the characters are mixing cocktails or whiskey-and-sodas and passing them to one another in a ritual of conviviality, sociability, and/or seduction. Coward used the social ritual of drinking as a way of demonstrating how people interact in various situations—encouraged or derailed by whatever they have happened to be drinking in the moment. He skillfully deployed cocktail parties, drunken binges, and ferocious hangovers in a wide range of dramatic situations.

In Coward's masterpiece, *Private Lives*, a divorced couple discovers each other once again on their new respective honeymoons, only to realize that they are still in love. Complications—and deep investigations into the nature of love and ego—ensue. Coward uses alcohol as a metaphor for these complex relationships; the male lead, Elyot, brings two Champagne cocktails out to the balcony, just as his former wife, Amanda, brings two Champagne cocktails out to her own adjoining balcony. Once they discover each other, they flee the hotel and their current spouses and escape to Paris. The Champagne cocktails are left to be discovered in their pristine state by the abandoned spouses and, of course, they raise a toast: "To absent friends."

In the second act, Amanda and Elyot settle down to a thoroughly inappropriate domesticity, rekindling their previous passion. A bottle of brandy, flourished with abandon, ignites their former argumentative relationship:

ELYOT: I think I mentioned once before that I have only had three minute liqueur glasses of brandy the whole evening long. A child of two couldn't get drunk on that.

AMANDA: On the contrary, a child of two could get violently drunk on only one glass of brandy.

ELYOT: Very interesting. How about a child of four, and a child of six, and a child of nine?

AMANDA: *(turning her head away)* Oh, do shut up.

ELYOT: *(witheringly)* We might get up a splendid little debate about that, you know, Intemperate Tots.

The most deeply Coward ever got involved with alcohol was probably in 1955, when he pulled yet another career out of his hat, this time as a cabaret performer in, of all places, the Desert Inn in Las Vegas. Dressed impeccably, as usual, in a tuxedo, he would pad up to the microphone in his blue velvet monogrammed slippers and entertain dozens of boozehounds of the highest order—Humphrey Bogart, Judy Garland, Frank Sinatra, among many other high rollers—with songs he had written for the British stage twenty or thirty years earlier. He was a smash hit, especially when he sang songs such as "I've Been to a Marvelous Party":

> **We knew the excitement was
>   bound to begin
> When Laura got blind on Dubonnet
>   and gin
> And scratched her veneer with a
>   Cartier pin.**

His cutting-edge audience, martinis set out in front of them, couldn't have liked it more.

COLE PORTER

I'm full of the old paprika,
I'm loaded with dynamite,
So come on down, come on down,
I'm throwing a ball tonight.
—"I'm Throwing a Ball"

In 1935, a reporter for the *New York Journal American* filed a besotted profile of Cole Porter, interviewed in the forty-first floor aerie of his apartment in the Waldorf Towers: "Writes close to twenty-five numbers for each show—then discards ten or so during rehearsals. Wears black tie with blue shirts. Likes Harlem. Can mix cocktails as dexterously as the best."

It's hardly surprising that Porter, the most successful Broadway composer-lyricist of the 1930s, was the top at mixing cocktails: he was the avatar of skill, elegance, and good manners. And there was nothing he liked more (or wrote about better) than a swell party.

Porter was born in 1892 in Peru, Indiana, the grandson of a very wealthy man. He went East to Yale, because it was expected of him, and thrived in its convivial and competitive environment. Porter developed a knack for writing songs and became a fan of Broadway, only a short train ride from New Haven. He antagonized his conventional grandfather by writing shows, but the initial reception of his work was so mortifying that Porter retreated to Europe in 1917. This provided a felicitous proving ground for his excellent manners and elevated tastes; by 1918, he had married a divorcée even richer than he, and the couple sojourned in Paris, Venice, and the Riviera throughout the 1920s, surrounded by very rarified company indeed.

Broadway superstars such as Irving Berlin and Richard Rodgers felt that Porter's prodigious talents were being wasted in Europe and lured

him back to New York in 1928, where Porter exploded upon the scene and had, pretty much, hit after hit in the 1930s. His influence was felt on bandstands and on the airwaves as well; his "Night and Day," introduced by Fred Astaire in *Gay Divorce* (1932—the film version, two years later, had a slightly different title), was one of the most popular songs of the first half of the twentieth century.

His life in New York revolved around the elegant apartment above the Waldorf Astoria that he shared with his wife, Linda. The apartment itself was a model of interior design and the Porters hosted many beautifully appointed dinner parties for world-renowned guests, with the best Champagne served by perfectly behaved butlers. Woe to the guest who overindulged—no more invitations were forthcoming. Porter knew his drinks: "Very few bottles of 1928 Champagne are good anymore," he lamented in 1948, "and as for 1921, it is so old and flat, people with country places only give it to their pigs."

His superb manners both hid and enabled his fear of confrontation; he would rather start over on a song than argue about it with a collaborator or producer. Nothing quite got Porter's dander up more than reviews that proposed "Porter's not up to his usual standard." He maintained that he had gone through years of scrapbooks that kept saying the same thing—when *was* his "usual standard"? He also felt that critics resented the fact that his was not a rags-to-riches story, but rather a riches-to-riches story; then again, his propensity for

The first of these, Du Barry Was a Lady, was a preposterous farce (involving a washroom attendant and time travel, I kid you not) but yielded some timeless classics, such as "Friendship" and "But in the Morning, No." It also featured a duet between Merman and Bert Lahr that apostrophized the kind of party that Porter himself was capable of throwing—parties appear in nearly a dozen Porter lyrics over the decade— "Well, Did You Evah!"

MERMAN: Well, did you evah!
What a swell party this is.
What Daiquiris!
What Sherry! Please!
What Burgundy!
What great Pommery!
What brandy, wow!
What whiskey, here's how!
What gin and what beer!

LAHR: Will you sober up, my dear?
Have you heard that Mrs. Cass
Had three beers and then ate
    the glass?

MERMAN: Well did you evah!
What a swell party this is.

giving engraved cigarette cases as opening-night presents and living so conspicuously well didn't do much to alter that perception.

Nearly everything changed for Porter in October 1937. While horseback riding at a tony club on Long Island, he had a terrible accident and both his legs were broken, his left leg so badly damaged that it required dozens of operations over the next two decades (and had to be amputated, eventually). Although the accident affected Porter's private life—he became addicted to painkillers and alcohol as time went on—it didn't seem to affect his workload (he did, however, become somewhat choosier about his projects) or the skill of his songwriting. From 1939 to 1943, he managed to compose not one, not two, but three hits in a row starring Ethel Merman.

If these lyrics strike the reader as familiar, it's because they were repurposed (and revised) for one of Porter's last projects, *High Society*, the 1956 film adaptation of *The Philadelphia Story*. In this case, a duet was tailored for two perfect (and antithetical) popular singing stars, Frank Sinatra and Bing Crosby, who, both in love with the same woman (Grace Kelly), find themselves drowning their sorrows together at a beautifully paneled bar (concealed in a den). "You must be one of the newer fellas," observes Crosby to Sinatra.

By the late Fifties, Porter was one of the older fellas. Still, with a glorious career behind him—and some lean years in front of him (he died in 1964)—Cole Porter knew the perfect ingredients to concoct a swell-egant, elegant party.

ELAINE STRITCH

Waiter, I'd like a bottle of vodka and a floor plan.
—**Elaine Stritch**

The turn of phrase "whiskey-voiced" is one that can be particularly flattering for the right actress. With Elaine Stritch, it was more than just a turn of phrase.

Stritch, as she was known to people who never even knew her, was in some ways a most unlikely star of the Broadway stage for the second half of the twentieth century. Not because she was old-fashioned, necessarily, but rather because she brought an old-school theatricality and unapologetic personality to a landscape that was growing increasingly dismissive to such panache and polish. She was born in 1925 to a conservative Catholic family outside of Detroit and would have been destined for a life in a convent or a country club (or, with her sheer will power, probably both) had the leggy blonde not caught the acting bug and moved to New York City in 1943. She was lucky enough—or clever enough—to study with some of New York's most imaginative and accomplished theater artists of the time. Stritch didn't attend the Actors Studio, although she ran in the same circles as many people who did, but attended instead the Dramatic Workshop program run by the German émigré director Erwin Piscator. She was also taught by Stella Adler, the doyenne of a deeply centered acting style.

This training imbued Stritch with a rare sense of theatrical truth. She always searched for specific, grounded, and intentional ways of creating a performance—but all that could be subsumed onstage in an instant by a larger theatrical truth, one that always gave audiences their money's worth by allowing them into the world of the show. Or, perhaps more correctly, Stritch carved a door into the fourth wall, cracked it open, and invited them in.

She was equally adept at serious (although not classical) drama as well as musical comedy. After some revue work, Stritch made a huge splash with a one-scene, one-song appearance in a groundbreaking 1952 revival of Rodgers and Hart's *Pal Joey* with her vermouth-dry rendition of "Zip." As a reporter recounting her interview with Gypsy Rose Lee, she brought the house down nightly. Turning serious, two seasons later, she triumphed in the original production of William Inge's *Bus Stop*, playing a disillusioned waitress in a greasy spoon, and rode out the 1950s with a mixture of unremarkable film, television, and summer-stock performances. She achieved over-the-title prestige in a mediocre 1958 musical called *Goldilocks*, but when she starred in Noël Coward's 1961 musical *Sail Away*, as the eternally resilient but skeptical hospitality director of an ocean liner, she earned herself the status accorded to Broadway royalty.

Coward was not one to suffer fools gladly—certainly not if they were headlining his first narrative musical on Broadway in many years. He knew the success of *Sail Away* rested on Stritch's star personality, which could steer this particular ship through any critical storm and safely into port. Coward was both respectful of her professional performance and annoyed at her personal anxiety on stage. "Fluffy and nervous inside," he called it. Truth be told, Stritch was always a handful. Sometimes, it was her drinking before a performance, when she needed a belt or two to fortify herself against her omnipresent anxiety; sometimes, it was even during a performance,

FOLLOWING SPREAD Stritch, who played alternate performances as Martha in Edward Albee's *Who's Afraid of Virginia Woolf?* in 1963, stepped into Albee's *A Delicate Balance*, as the hard-drinking sister, Claire, thirty-three years later.

when she would sneak in a cocktail or two. Once, according to Alexandra Jacobs's sterling biography, *Still Here*, when Stritch was performing the role of Martha in matinees of *Who's Afraid of Virginia Woolf?*, she left backstage in her bra and girdle, threw on a raincoat, and ran to the corner bar for some Dutch courage. (She had been told Coward himself was in the audience that afternoon.). Stritch would often equivocate about how much she was actually drinking at any one time, even if it was apparent to her collaborators and coworkers; she was certainly in denial about how much she needed to drink. But, to be fair, Coward—a disciplinarian of the first order when it came to making sure that everything was shipshape on his shows—never complained that alcohol got in the way of her star turn in his musical, which she played in for many months in New York and London.

Was Stritch difficult? Well, that's a very shopworn word when it comes to actors. Was she determined to make sure that everything she did on stage was truthful, practical, and particular? Absolutely. Did she drive her collaborators to distraction in her quest for such particularity? It depends on the collaborator. Did she have a highly subjective view on how theater and stardom were supposed to work, blurring the lines between onstage performance and offstage performance? You bet. Was she always determined to be the center of attention? Waiter, bring me a double. But, for many, Stritch represented an old-school, no-nonsense, foul-mouthed directness that many found refreshing and that audiences found intoxicating.

In 1970, for the musical *Company*, she found her perfect role in the supporting part of Joanne, a divorcée married "three or four times," a resident of the Upper East Side, a neighborhood that Stritch herself would eventually inhabit at the Carlyle Hotel in legendary fashion. Although the part of Joanne was not written *for* her by book writer George Furth and composer-lyricist

Stephen Sondheim, it was certainly written *on* her. Furth came to know her back when he was an actor in the Fifties and Sixties; when he was drinking and she was drinking, they often reveled together. Through a haze several liters thick, Furth recounted an evening when he, Stritch, Jack Cassidy, and Gig Young went drinking together; it boggles the mind.

Stritch stayed with *Company* for over a year of its New York run and then on tour throughout the country, growing in stature and getting a higher salary and better billing. When she played Joanne on the West End during the musical's transfer, it was a veritable homecoming; London took Stritch and her unpretentious raucous personality to heart and she moved there for the next decade to perform on stage and on television.

When she returned to the States in the early eighties, she transitioned into a living legend. Stritch performed in numerous benefits and concerts always to the tune of her own inimitable timing and vocal idiosyncrasies. Even if the appearances were brief and transitory, it hardly mattered—her growling, eyebrow-raising delivery could bring full houses to a grinding halt. Eventually, she grew weary of being a featured cameo act in various concerts, variety shows, and television programs and developed a one-woman show about the subject that interested her most: herself. *Elaine Stritch At Liberty* opened first downtown at the Public Theater's cabaret space, but a Broadway transfer was inevitable, and in 2001, she enchanted audiences with the somewhat embroidered story of her climb to fame. It's an understatement to say that one had to take her performed autobiography with a pinch of salt—a pillar should have been ordered up.

Nevertheless, when Elaine Stritch passed away at the age of 89 in 2014, Broadway knew that it had lost perhaps the last of a rare breed—the no-nonsense dame who would give a 110% of herself to make sure that audiences left the theater buzzing—about her. Stritch's drinking was always a part of her personality, whether she wanted it to be or not. Some of that was a lack of discretion; at one point in the late 1960s, to make ends meet—she claimed—she tended bar at the famous nightspot Elaine's (no relation). Some of her reputation was due to the fact that she appeared in plays by Tennessee Williams (*Small Craft Warnings*) and Edward Albee (*Who's Afraid of Virginia Woolf?*, *A Delicate Balance*), as well as Neil Simon's *The Gingerbread Lady*, and,

of course, *Company*, that actually required her character to be in her cups for most of the performance. And some of it was simply the notion that it was in character for her to have an intimate relationship with alcohol. That seemed to be part of the package, and no matter how hard Stritch worked to get completely sober, as time went on, sobriety seemed like miscasting—at least as far as her public persona was concerned.

And one miscast Elaine Stritch at one's peril.

LEFT Plus a little jest: Elaine Stritch has another round as Joanne in *Company*, before launching into her big number, "The Ladies Who Lunch."

TENNESSEE WILLIAMS

A hot bath and a long cold drink always
give me a brand-new outlook on life!
—*A Streetcar Named Desire*

To appropriate the kind of metaphor that was Tennessee Williams's touch of genius, if most plays that involved drinking liquor were drawing-room comedies that put a Chinese paper lantern over alcohol's rude remarks or vulgar actions, Williams ripped the lantern off and exposed the sharp glaring realities of drinking—good and plain.

In Tennessee Williams's plays, drink is fairly ubiquitous and rarely charming. This honesty would have come naturally to Thomas Lanier Williams, who not only grew up in a household with a drinker, but also went on to become, alas, quite a drinker himself. In terms of the arc of his career, one might well quote the title song from *Cabaret*, "Well, that's what comes of too much pills and liquor."

Williams was born in 1911 in Columbus, Mississippi, and spent much of his youth torn between the traditions of the South, the complexities of his dysfunctional family, and his deeply aspirant, poetic nature. He had an itinerant youth—indeed, his entire life was extremely peripatetic—but by the time World War II ended, he had established himself as a first-rate poet, a screenplay writer, and an up-and-coming dramatist, with the 1943 Broadway production of *The Glass Menagerie*. By the time the 1940s were over, he, along with Arthur Miller, represented a new kind of playwright who smashed the conventions of American drama and led not only the theater but also the country into a future of psychological acuity, sexual complexity, and deep, if not always pleasant, honesty.

If liquor did much eventually to tarnish the career of Tennessee Williams, its skillful deployment in the plays he wrote helped burnish its effect and deliver truthfulness to audiences around the world. Nearly all of Williams's plays involve alcohol in some way. Both *The Glass Menagerie* (otherwise fairly benign in its alcoholic content) and *Sweet Bird of Youth* involve huge hangover scenes; in the latter, the first drink that's served as the play begins is a Bromo-seltzer via room service. Several plays feature rundown hotels or resorts with full bar service, and in *Cat in a Hot Tin Roof*, Williams creates one of the protean inebriates of American drama, the failed football star Brick, who drowns his sorrows and disappointments by crawling into the bottle until

LEFT Tennessee Williams had the unique opportunity to fill in for another actor as Doc, a waterfront inebriate, in his own play, *Small Craft Warnings*, for a few weeks during its Off-Broadway run in 1972.

he hears an existential "click." As his frustrated wife, Maggie, puts it, Brick spends his time "devoting yourself to the occupation of drinkin'!"

By the time the 1950s were over, Williams had claimed his right to be called America's finest living playwright. He was also an extremely accomplished poet, the winner of one Tony Award and two Pulitzer Prizes for drama, an essayist, and an outspoken, if infrequent, critic of American hypocrisy. Of course, he himself was a character of extraordinary and colorful public recognition. Although he was protected and promoted by various agents and hangers-on throughout his career, to my knowledge, he never had a publicity agent. If there was anyone for whom a publicity agent was superfluous, it was Tennessee Williams—despite an innate shyness, publicity seem to be his second nature, and television talk shows were his confessional.

After *The Night of the Iguana* in 1961, however, Williams's career trajectory charted downward. Ironically, the freedoms and nonconformity that Williams brought to the American stage somewhat outpaced him in real life. He had great difficulty re-creating the success of the previous two decades, and his projects came to be as self-indulgent as his personal life. Although drinking was part of his life—red wine and vodka usually, Brandy Alexanders for a treat—he managed to avoid putting an actual bar on stage until 1972. *Small Craft Warnings* was a kind of *Iceman Cometh* with a beachfront locale. Set in a crummy bar overlooking the Pacific Ocean somewhere near San Diego, it is inhabited by a "community club" of barflies and tortured losers for whom life following the turbulent 1960s has come too late and too soon. It included language and situations that, even by 1972, would have been untouchable by Hollywood.

The play didn't even open on Broadway—it opened at a theater on the Bowery, an irony not lost on Williams—and, since it didn't get the best reviews, at one point there was the need to drum up publicity. When the actor playing Doc, a drunken doctor who has lost his license to practice, stepped out for a few weeks, his role was played by Williams himself. Apparently, he was pretty good in the part, except when he started to invent lines on his own. This may, of course, have confused the other actors—one member of the cast said that when Williams's lips stopped moving, it was time to say your own lines—but surely this was a writer's prerogative. Unfortunately, this stunt would go awry when Williams would frequently show up to the theater zonked on pills and liquor. He was particularly incensed that *Small Craft Warnings*

was doing such lousy business that it was about to be kicked out of its Off-Broadway theater and replaced by, of all things, a Noël Coward musical review. Williams had known and befriended Coward for decades. In fact, during a visit to Italy in the 1950s, Williams who was a notoriously bad driver, almost killed both of them while careening along the Italian roads—but that didn't stop him from saying horrendous things about Coward and his work while lurching about onstage performing the role of Doc.

By that point in his career, nothing surprised audiences or journalists about Tennessee Williams. His last Broadway play, in 1980, was about F. Scott Fitzgerald and Fitzgerald's wife, Zelda. Entitled *Clothes for a Summer Hotel*, it was an elegiac look at loss and love and memory and reputation and expectation—all the things that Tennessee Williams wrote about so well in his prime. The fact that he brought two of American literature's most immortal alcoholics to the Broadway stage is worth contemplating. Perhaps he was grabbing that torch for himself—a way of hearing the "click" in his head, which, as Brick said, makes him peaceful.

BELOW In a small-town hotel room, surrounded by what the *New York Times* called "comic squalor," Paul Newman and Geraldine Page wake up to the morning after in Williams's 1959 play, *Sweet Bird of Youth*.

THE LITTLE GREEN SNAKE

(inspired by *Ah, Wilderness!* [1933] and *Take Me Along* [1958])

Eugene O'Neill's *Ah, Wilderness!* was an alternate reality of his own upbringing. It is the coming-of-age story of Richard Miller, who's fully supported by a loving family. Still, the shadow of alcohol falls on the play. Richard's Uncle Sid is a jovial reprobate, but always falling off the wagon, much to his family's dismay.

When the play was musicalized in 1958 by composer/lyricist Bob Merrill as *Take Me Along*, Uncle Sid, a gave young Richard a guided tour of the hangover landscape. In "Little Green Snake," Sid sings:

> *Did see my green snake, my little green snake?*
> *Did see the green man*
> *And the tattooed Indian'?*
> *Now did you know their names are "Muck" and "Merkle"?*
> *See, I know that 'cause I'm in the inner circle.*
> *I am one of them, and now you're one of us.*

When *Take Me Along* opened on Broadway, producer David Merrick had the genius idea to cast Jackie Gleason as Uncle Sid. They bickered constantly, and Gleason demanded the largest weekly salary ever given to a Broadway performer. Merrick gave "The Great One" the princely sum of $5,050—fifty dollars more than the previous record-holder and Gleason shuffled away with a Tony Award. How sweet it was.

**MARTINI
+ COCTAIL SHAKER**

2 ounces vodka
1 ounce dry vermouth
Lime peel, cut as long
 and curly as possible

Chill a martini glass by putting it in the freezer for about 5 minutes.
Add the vodka and vermouth to a cocktail shaker; shake well and strain into the
martini glass. Finish off by adding your "little green snake"—the lime peel.

THE MASTER'S MARTINI AND THE BULLSHOT

(Inspired by Noël Coward)

In the 1920s, Noël Coward's personal predilection was for a martini. It was considered *au fait* to mix as dry a martini as possible—that is, one that favored far more gin over vermouth. Coward was quoted as saying, "A perfect Martini should be made by filling a glass with gin, then waving it in the general direction of Italy." He may have been riffing off a similar remark ascribed to his chum, Winston Churchill: "I would like to observe the vermouth from across the room while I drink my martini."

At some point in the Sixties, the playwright switched to a fashionable drink of the period called the Bullshot, invented in the mid-1950s at The Caucus Club in Detroit when a Campbell's Soup executive wanted a way to sell more beef consommé.

Coward would drink the Bullshot for the rest of his life. When the Queen Mother came to visit Coward for lunch at his Jamaica estate in 1965, he introduced her to the drink: "She had two and was delighted."

MASTER'S MARTINI

MARTINI

- **2 ounces gin (Hemingway liked Gordon's)**
- **½ ounce (tops!) dry vermouth**
- **Either one olive or three on a toothpick—an even number is considered bad luck**

Chill a martini glass with ice in the fridge for 10 minutes while you fill another glass with ice and gin. Stir well. When you're absolutely ready, swish the martini glass with vermouth, then add the gin, strained. Stir again lightly, and add olive.

THE BULLSHOT

COPPER MUG (OR ANY GLASS) + COCKTAIL SHAKER

- **1½ ounces vodka**
- **3 ounces chilled beef bouillon**
- **1 dash Worcestershire sauce**
- **4 drops Tabasco**
- **1 squeeze lemon juice (at least!)**
- **Salt, pepper, and celery salt**

Pop some ice cubes into a cocktail shaker, add all the ingredients, and shake for six to eight seconds. Strain into a copper mug, if you have one, although a glass will do the trick. Serve with impeccable manners.

THE OLD-FASHIONED

(Inspired by *Panama Hattie*, 1940)

Although synonymous with high society, Porter contributed one of the greatest saloon songs of all time. It was tailored for Ethel Merman in the 1940 musical *Panama Hattie*. Merman played a saloon owner named Hattie Maloney who sets up shop in the Canal Zone of Panama City. As Porter once wrote, "I'd rather write for Ethel than anyone else in the world."

The old-fashioned dates as far back as the mid-nineteenth century. Some mavens think they got a little fussy in the way ingredients were added during Prohibition and after, but Porter—and Merman—play it straight.

So, make it another old-fashioned, please

Leave out the cherry

Leave out the orange

Leave out the bitters

Just make it straight rye.

LOWBALL
+ MUDDLER

Sugar cube

2 drops Angostura bitters

1 splash club soda

2½ ounces rye (some people use bourbon, but let's follow Cole Porter)

1 orange slice

1 cherry (a nice bourbon-soaked one, please; nothing radioactively red)

Using a lowball glass, soak the sugar cube with bitters, add the club soda, and muddle to make a light syrup. Add the rye, orange, cherry, and some ice—unless you leave them out, of course. Stir gently.

— WHAT'S A MUDDLER? —

A muddler is a blunt-edged tool used to mash ingredients together in the bottom of a glass. If you don't have a muddler, don't worry—you can use the butt end of a wooden spoon.

THE VODKA STINGER

(Inspired by *Company*, 1970)

◇

Another chance to disapprove;
Another brilliant zinger.
Another reason not to move;
Another vodka stinger!
I'll drink to that.

It's probably safe to assume that more show-tune fans have heard about vodka stingers than have actually tried them; such is the fame of Stephen Sondheim's catalogue of the discontented, "The Ladies Who Lunch" from *Company*.

Sondheim said that every number in *Company* is about marriage—"except one." This song is a veritable time capsule of what ladies of leisure with a certain economic privilege in New York's Upper East Side did with their spare time (of which they had plenty): dabble in highbrow art, of which they had little understanding (Mahler, Pinter, "optical" art—as if there's any other kind). When Elaine Stritch was first given the song by Sondheim, she wondered if "a piece of Mahler" was some kind a pastry that you snacked on.

The stinger was originally a brandy- or Cognac-based drink, deployed most often as a nightcap, but vodka eventually replaced brandy. One wag, conversant with the diurnal rhythms of the cocktail lounge, once concluded, "What goes with a stinger? Another stinger." He and Joanne would have made good drinking buddies.

CORDIAL
+ COCKTAIL SHAKER

1½ ounces vodka
1 ounce crème de menthe (I prefer the clear-ish version; the green stuff reminds me of cough syrup.)

1 mint sprig, for garnish
Cracked ice

Fill the cocktail shaker with the cracked ice. Pour the liquid ingredients over the ice.
As the August 1948 *Esquire* put it, "Shake with cracked ice until shaker frosts. Strain."
Garnish with a mint sprig, if you like.

A SIDECAR NAMED DESIRE

(Inspired by *A Streetcar Named Desire*, 1947)

Williams's hothouse of a play—by turns erotic and explosive—is one of the great game-changers of the American stage, and one can easily interpret Williams's use of alcohol as a symbolic through line. The working-class mechanic Stanley Kowalski only drinks beer—even when his wife, Stella, gives birth, he celebrates by showering himself not with Champagne but a geyser of beer. His nemesis, Blanche DuBois, claims to enjoy a nice Coca-Cola with crushed ice, but her preference is for a covert swig or two or three of Southern Comfort; secret drinking for a secret life.

The sidecar is time-honored drink. Its base, Cognac, is a nice reference to Blanche's pretensions ("DuBois … it's a French name."). The addition of Peychaud's bitters is a nod to the play's New Orleans setting, where Antoine Peychaud created his "American Aromatic Bitters" decades before the Civil War. Sometimes, there's a dash so quickly.

MARTINI
+ COCTAIL SHAKER

¾ ounce Cognac
(it doesn't have to be a pricey brand)

¾ ounce triple sec
(I like Pierre Ferrand orange liqueur)

¾ ounce lemon juice

Lemon peel

Light brown sugar

1 or 2 dashes
Peychaud's bitters

Frost a martini glass by putting it in the freezer for 5 minutes. Pour a small mound of the sugar onto a plate. When frosted, take the glass out of the freezer, rub the lemon peel around the rim of the glass just enough to make it moist, then dip the rim in the sugar. In the shaker, add ice; combine the Cognac, triple sec, and lemon juice; Shake (for a count of ten), then strain the ingredients into the glass and finish with a dash or two of bitters; let the bitters float through the drink.

— LOUISIANA PURCHASE —

For many years, one could only purchase Peychaud's bitters in Louisiana. Luckily, it has now become readily available. The firm also sells a whisky-based version that's nearly as expensive as a bottle of whisky, but it's exquisite.

CHAPTER 4

Faraway Places

WHERE THE SKY MEETS THE SEA

Sir Charles came from a sanitorium
And yelled for drinks in my emporium.
I mixed one drink—he's in memoriam
To keep my love alive.
— *A Connecticut Yankee*

A full bottle of Champagne could well be a passport to Fantasyland. In the 1927 musical *A Connecticut Yankee*, with a score by Rodgers and Hart, one character takes this far too literally.

In this updated treatment of Mark Twain's 1889 novel, the lead character, Martin, is clocked on the head with a full bottle of Champagne by a jealous girlfriend. In his dazzled delusions, he imagines himself back in the days of King Arthur's Court, replete with enchantresses and wizards. Complications ensue, but so do some Rodgers and Hart classics, such as "My Heart Stood Still" and "Thou Swell."

Liquor's magical ability to transport one to another time and place goes back to the potions and medicinal drinks of ancient Greece. Shakespeare loved to concoct some potion or other while concocting a plot—Oberon creates a mystical love potion to create havoc in *A Midsummer Night's Dream,* and Juliet is slipped a "cordial" that allows her to awake from the dead. The creators of *West Side Story* wisely skipped that one, but keeping much of the adult action centered on Doc's drugstore is, I suppose, a nod to the pharmacological folderol found in Shakespeare.

THERE'S SIMPLY NOT A MORE CONGENIAL SPOT

Mythical kingdoms and cultures feature heavily in opera and the occasional operetta, but by the time Rodgers and Hart tackled their version of Camelot in 1927, this kind of fantasy setting was more useful for comedy than for, say, an exercise in Wagnerian passions. Rodgers and Hart tackled the show again in 1943, updating the source material one more time, now to the contemporaneous era of World War II. The bang on the head with the Champagne bottle occurred again, but the songwriting team beefed up the role of the evil enchantress Morgan Le Fay for their muse, Vivienne Segal, giving her an unforgettable catalogue of her serial homicides, "To Keep My Love Alive."

When Alan Jay Lerner and Frederick Loewe took up Camelot in a more serious and lyrical vein seventeen years later, they had to contend with the mists of ridicule whipped up by Rodgers and Hart—but they created an enduring classic (and, of course, the sublime transitioned back to the ridiculous

with *Monty Python's Spamalot*). Lerner, along with lyricist "Yip" Harburg, was one of Broadway's more reliable fabulists, happy to venture to a romantic spot—real or imagined—without irony or cynicism.

Lerner and Loewe's first big hit, in 1947, was *Brigadoon,* an original tale of a mythical town in the Highlands of Scotland that, through a miracle is kept, amberlike, in its eighteenth-century state, only to emerge from the mists for one day every hundred years. Two New Yorkers—one romantic, one cynical—stumble upon this enchanted town while hiking in the Highlands. Of course, when the reality of Brigadoon hits them, the cynical friend believes too much whiskey is involved,

while his more romantic pal heeds the call of a simpler time and place as well as the lovely lass who lives there.

ONE SHORT DAY IN THE EMERALD CITY

Enchanted lands have their appeal on Broadway— the Arabian bazaars of *Kismet* and *Aladdin;* Candide's Eldorado; the island of *Once on This Island;* the undersea kingdom of *The Little Mermaid;* the Francophile wherever of *Beauty and the Beast;* the magical forest of *Into the Woods; Xanadu;* SpongeBob's Bikini Bottom—but, of course, this is the kind of thing that Hollywood has the resources to do better. Still, there's one enchanted land that

has captivated Broadway repeatedly since the early days of the twentieth century: Oz.

The Wizard of Oz's creator, L. Frank Baum, adapted his book to the musical stage two years after it was published; opening at Broadway's Majestic Theatre in 1903, it ran for almost 300 performances. It practically vanished as a viable show by the 1920s, but the production staff of the 1939 film version knew the original musical well enough to borrow aspects of it for the Hollywood version. That adaptation, of course, cast a very long shadow, inspiring two extraordinary successful "takes" on the Oz legend: the all-Black version, *The Wiz,* in 1975, and *Wicked,*

which provides backstory on the original book and is still going strong. A stage version of the movie, too, touched down briefly at Madison Square Garden in 1988, with Eartha Kitt playing the Wicked Witch of the West.

Wicked witches were comparatively benign as the twenty-first century got underway, as enchanted lands and fantasy subjects on Broadway got a little darker. There had always been characters from the Great Beyond in various plays and musicals, usually materializing on stage to bring some mortal character into another realm. There was the eponymous *I Married an Angel,* the Devil and Lola from *Damn*

ABOVE In the 1980 revival of *Brigadoon,* Tommy Albright (played by Martin Vidnovic) gets a heavy dose of modern civilization from his pal, Jeff Douglas (Mark Zimmerman); whether Scotch and soda was consumed is open to question.

ABOVE Mr. Addams,
I give you a toast: a
potent draught is raised
in the Addams family
manse to welcome a
"normal" family who
came to see 'em. From
the Phoenix national tour
of *The Addams Family*.

Yankees, and Noël Coward's enchanted Elvira, a deceased first wife who wants nothing so much as to bring her living husband, Charles, with her up to Home Sweet Heaven in innumerable revivals of *Blithe Spirit* as well as its musical avatar, *High Spirits*. But those spiritual interventions were whimsical compared to *Ghost the Musical, Shrek, Matilda the Musical, Frozen, King Kong, Harry Potter and the Cursed Child, Beetlejuice*, and *Hadestown*. In *The Addams Family*, not only did the kreepy and kooky family proceed in their mysterious and ooky ways, but several singing-and-dancing cadavers from the Addams dynasty also made their appearance and a bewitching potion was introduced, as way

of Pugsley getting back at his sister, Wednesday; it was supposed to reveal one's darker nature.

In much the same way, cocktails moved into darker territory after World War II (as did much of the sober world, too), with such provocative brews as the Green Devil, the Night Shade, the Scorpion, the Vampire, and the Dracula. These were pretty much one-shot novelties, but the Dark 'n Stormy, the Corpse Reviver (Nos. 1 and 2), the Bloody Mary, and the Zombie have taken their place in bars, nightspots, and liquor cabinets across the country. They're all excellent drinks, although the Zombie is not for all comers: insert "lethal damage to the brain" joke as you will.

HERE AM I, YOUR SPECIAL ISLAND

The most famous enchanted island in Broadway history is based on a real one: Bali Ha'i, from the 1949 Rodgers and Hammerstein's *South Pacific*. When James Michener was stationed as a naval officer in the South Pacific during World War II, he made a note in his journal about a village called Bali-ha'i. The name stuck, but it seemed to him far more appropriate to append it to an emerging volcanic island off the coast of Espiritu Santo called Aoba: "Like a jewel, it could be perceived in one loving glance.... Like most lovely things, one had to seek it out and even to know what one was seeking before it could be found."

When Michener's *Tales of the South Pacific* was adapted into a musical by Rodgers, Hammerstein, and Joshua Logan, Bali Ha'i took on a life of its own. The creative team amped up the appeal of Bali Ha'i from Michener's original version (it was an island that took most of the young women of the area for their protection and was supervised by a Catholic Mother Superior) into a kind of tropical Las Vegas. As Luther Billis spins its appeal to the reluctant Lieutenant Cable: "But, another thing goes on over there—the ceremonial of the boar's tooth. After they kill the boar, they pass around some of that coconut liquor and women dance with just their skirts on (his voice becoming evil) and everybody gets to know everybody pretty well."

Cable winds up succumbing not just to the charms of Bali Ha'i, but particularly to the charms of a beautiful young woman named Liat; it proves to be his ultimate undoing—love, not coconut liquor, turns out to be the ultimate intoxicant.

Still, in *South Pacific*, the most intoxicating moment comes not from any kind of ceremony but from the sincere and tremulous sharing of two glasses of Cognac between the sophisticated French planter Emile de Becque and the more naïve and intimidated American nurse, Nellie Forbush. There's something ineffably romantic in that simple gesture and when the orchestra swells with the full emotionalism of Richard Rodgers's music, one can practically smell the enchanted aroma of the Cognac itself. Who can explain it, who can tell you why?

In all of these enchanted musicals, everyone usually finds their own "special island"—a place of spiritual and emotional bliss. Of course, if you find yourself on a special island—in a lounge chair or a hammock, with a mai tai or Scorpion within reach—that makes for some enchanted afternoon.

FOLLOWING SPREAD In *South Pacific* (1949), plantation owner Emile de Becque (here played by Paulo Szot in the Lincoln Center Theatre revival, 2007) offers Nellie Forbush (Kelli O'Hara) her first cognac; some enchanted evenings ensue.

THE HEATHER ON THE HILL

(Inspired by *Brigadoon*, 1947)

Quick Broadway quiz: *Brigadoon* has a scene in a swanky New York bar: Yes or no? If you answered "No," that would make sense; after all, the musical is about a long-lost Scottish village in the mists of the Highlands. But, alas, you would be wrong. Much to the chagrin of set designers everywhere, Alan Jay Lerner set a scene late in Act Two in a swanky New York bar. There the hero, Tommy, has a rendezvous with his fiancée, Jane—a grasping socialite, whose sniping only offers up sound cues to lyrics that evoke Brigadoon for Tommy—and soon he is off to the Highlands again for a happy ending.

A cocktail inspired by *Brigadoon* would have to include Scotch, of course—although locals there refer to it as "whisky." This drink is modeled on the Rusty Nail, which emerged as a simple but potent cocktail in the early 1960s. Drambuie is a wondrous liqueur from the Isle of Skye, which is Scotch whisky sent one more time through the distillery with "heather honey" and other spices. The branch of thyme is not purely decorative (to suggest heather), but adds, shall we say, a nice burr to the mixture.

**LOWBALL
(OLD FASHIONED)**

Orange peel
**1¼ ounces blended
Scotch (Dewar's
blends beautifully in
a cocktail)**

¾ ounce Drambuie
1 stalk of thyme

Place ice in the glass. Rub an orange peel around the rim and drop it in the glass.
Add the Scotch and Drambuie and stir gently. Add the thyme.
You'll have a wonderful thyme and friends will wish they were there.

─ **THE PERFECT BLENDSHIP** ─

Scotch is a tricky addition to any cocktail; its distinctive taste can often be
denatured by embellishments. Any cocktail made with Scotch should use a blended whiskey
rather than a single malt, which, on its own, is marvelous, but not in a mixed cocktail.
All a good single malt needs is one ice cube.

DEFYING GRAVITY

(inspired by *Wicked*, 2004)

To paraphrase a famous saying, "It's not easy drinking green." Although it's not so bad for health juices, the color is a little more difficult to swallow when it's in the liquor department. Artificially colored beer might be okay for St. Patrick's Day (if you must), but one should tread lightly with green-colored drinks. Crème de menthe is a perfectly respectable drink; the green version has been, traditionally, a mixture of natural mint leaves and some enhancements. It was very popular in the early twentieth century, but lately the clearer version is considered more sophisticated and has become more accepted. It also has a more subtle taste, in my opinion.

The Defying Gravity cocktail allows the reader to "greenify" their cocktail according to their own tint predilections. Its basis is green Chartreuse (there's also a yellow version), a liqueur that dates back to the seventeenth century. Made by French monks from a secret recipe, it comprises more than 130 herbs. The color chartreuse apparently derives its name from the liqueur, not the other way around.

Of course, in *Wicked*, there's a green elixir that's a special secret recipe of its own; one could go into further detail, but that would be telling. In the meantime, give this Chartreuse-based elixir a try. Probably after one—and certainly after two—your cares will melt away.

CORDIAL
+ COCKTAIL SHAKER

1¼ ounces green
    Chartreuse
¾ ounce vodka
1 dash mint bitters

Chill a cordial glass by putting it in the freezer for 5 minutes. In a cocktail shaker, mix
the Chartreuse and vodka with ice. Strain into a cordial glass.
Add a dash of mint bitters—or more if you like—to get your cocktail to
the right shade of green (your call). Stir gently, then take flight.

THE DEAD THING

(Inspired by *Beetlejuice*, 2019)

As cocktail recipes go, the Corpse Reviver has been lying around for a long time. In his seminal 1941 *Cocktail Guide and Ladies' Companion*, Crosby Gaige takes specific note of its qualities: "Of this, one will revive any self-respecting corpse—four taken in swift succession will return corpse to reclining position."

The Corpse Reviver has been reported in various accounts as making its debut in London in the mid-nineteenth century; it eventually made its journey across the pond by 1900 and became a stimulating method of reviving one's self after a hangover: "hair of the dog" and all that. There is a Corpse Reviver No. 1, but it has been interred back into the vault in favor of the No. 2, which is crisper but no less powerful.

The name, obviously, seems appropriate for a Beetlejuice cocktail, as the plot of the musical revolves so intently around escaping the Netherworld and finding the humanity in departed spirits. This concoction may have you calling out for it three times—do so at the risk of your immortal soul.

COUPE
+ COCKTAIL SHAKER
+ ATOMIZER

1 ounce gin (I recommend Tanqueray Rangpur)

1 ounce Lillet Rouge

1 ounce triple sec or curacao

1 ounce lemon juice

Two sprays of absinthe (or Pernod or Absente—a 100 ml bottle of Absente is reasonably priced and goes a long way)

Chill a coupe glass by placing it in the freezer for 5 minutes. Fill the cocktail shaker with ice, then the gin, Lillet, triple sec, and lemon juice. Fill an atomizer with absinthe and spray the inside of the coupe glass twice. Strain the shaker into the glass and keep your eye out for sand worms.

— WHAT IS AN ATOMIZER? —

Originally created to spritz vermouth into martinis, an atomizer is a small metal pump sprayer that spritzes a tiny amount of liquor into a glass. If you don't have an atomizer, just pour a very small amount of the ingredient to be atomized in the glass, swirl it around to coat, and pour out the excess.

BALI HA'I MA'I TA'I

(Inspired by *South Pacific*, 1949)

The most obvious cocktail inspired by *South Pacific* would be a Bloody Mary, but this concoction weaves in the mythical and the local, creating the kind of tropical drink that calls out to you—and indeed has called out to generations of Americans—to come away.

Although there had been "tropical" drinks before World War II, the explosion of their popularity can be traced to the creation of the mai tai by Victor "Trader Vic" Bergeron at his Oakland bar around 1944. Rum-based drinks with various additions—lime, pineapple, juices, syrups, and embellishments—soon sprang up in imitation (and in frequent dilution of the mai tai's original intent).

The postwar period saw a boom in bringing Polynesian culture—or a stereotypical appropriation of it—back to the States. Indeed, tiki lamps and tiki shirts and tiki record albums were a major fad of the Fifties, especially when Hawaii became a state in 1959.

Thankfully, the mai tai is here to stay, even if the music of Lex Baxter and backyard luau parties have receded into the low-flying clouds of the past.

**TALL (HIGHBALL)
OR TIKI GLASS
+ COCKTAIL SHAKER**

3 ounces light rum
(unflavored)
½ ounce triple sec
½ teaspoon L'Orgeat
almond liqueur
½ ounce lime juice

½ teaspoon sugar
1 mint sprig
1 brandied cherry
1 lime slice
1 pineapple stick
1 cocktail umbrella

If you are using a highball class, chill it by putting it in the freezer for 5 minutes. Pour the rum, triple sec, L'Orgeat, lime juice, and sugar into a cocktail shaker and add ice. Take the glass out of the freezer and add cracked ice then strain the contents of the shaker into the glass. Garnish with a mint sprig, slightly torn to release its flavor and whatever garnish theatrics your heart desires: I suggest a cherry, lime slice, and pineapple stick speared together on a cocktail umbrella (Why not? What else are you going to use them for?). This is enough flavor for any tropical drink; you don't need additional juice(s).

INTERMISSION: FLOPS WITH A FLIP

Musicals have always upped the ante by using celebratory drinking as way of making things more dramatic, building numbers around raising a glass or two at a pub or a nightclub.

But from the mid-1950s to the end of the 1960s, it seemed as if every other musical had some number in which characters either drank in public or watched people who did. Three middle-range hits of the period—*Flower Drum Song*, *Do Re Mi*, and *Little Me*—had big nightclub scenes and three more—*New Girl in Town*, *Man of La Mancha*, and *Zorbà*—provided the requisite boisterous tavern setting. Perhaps 1970's *Applause* was the end of an era; it at least turned a corner, featuring the first Broadway musical number set in a gay bar.

Still, those were the hits—or at least shows with a respectable run. For certain musicals not as fortunate to get long runs or make their money back or win awards, there was an almost obligatory inclusion of some kind of alcoholic frolic, chorus boys and girls included at no extra charge. If it felt desperate at times, well, that was part of the fun.

Here then are a few flops with a flip (a liquor-based drink, fortified with egg and sugar). Alas, the list doesn't include *Pousse-Café*, a 1966 bomb based on the German classic film, *The Blue Angel*. This show, named after a multi-layered after-dinner cocktail, was such a disaster—one performance, despite a score by Duke Ellington—that it didn't even leave a decent production photo.

BEN FRANKLIN IN PARIS (1964)

A few years before *1776* opened, Ben Franklin got his own musical, with Robert Preston *(right)* impersonating the great patriot and inventor during his stint as an ambassador. This sprightly number, "God Bless the Human Elbow," celebrated the joint's ability to bring a tankard to one's lips. There were also a bunch of French monks singing "In vino veritas" as a back-up chorus.

HIGH SPIRITS (1964)

Based on Noël Coward's *Blithe Spirit*, in addition to referring to alcoholic spirits in its title, the musical has several scenes where cocktails are used as a lubricant to the Great Beyond. Here Beatrice Lillie, as the psychic Madame Arcati, toasts the possibilities of the spirit world.

BREAKFAST AT TIFFANY'S (1966)

It featured two major talents of the 1960s—Richard Chamberlain and Mary Tyler Moore—in their intended Broadway musical debuts, but, alas, it never officially opened in New York and went down in history as one of the most notorious flops of all time. That, however, did not stop the show from having its obligatory musical number at the top of Act Two where the heroine (Holly Golightly—the musical was called *Holly Golightly* for about ten minutes) dances on the bar while being worshipped by members of the chorus.

SHERRY! (1967)

Another titular intoxicant, this musical refers to Sheridan Whiteside, the acidulous celebrity at the center of Kaufman and Hart's *The Man Who Came to Dinner*. Dolores Gray, as one of Whiteside's actress acolytes, gets her requisite number in a bar (in Ohio, no less) and also gets her own solo number celebrating her pal—"Sherry!"—where, inevitably, she refers to him as "intoxicating."

HER FIRST ROMAN (1968)

It actually had a number called "In Vino Veritas" with a lot of Roman soldiers quaffing Egyptian wine from a lot of gold-sprayed goblets supplied by the props department. Based on *Caesar and Cleopatra*, a play by George Bernard Shaw (hey, it worked once!), the musical had, at least, two stellar performers in Richard Kiley and Leslie Uggams, who played the title characters.

CHAPTER 5

Watering Holes

RIGHT THIS WAY, YOUR TABLE'S WAITING

———————————◇———————————

Come blow your horn, start celebrating—
Right this way, your table's waiting.
—"Cabaret" by John Kander and Fred Ebb

Whatever else you might say about Shakespeare—and there's a lot to be said, most of it good—he knew how to set a scene.

At the very end of the sixteenth century, he wrote two plays—*Henry IV, Parts One* and *Two*—and created the first tavern scene in the English-speaking theater: the Boar's Head Inn in Eastcheap, as a locale for the roistering adventures of Prince Hal, Sir John Falstaff, Doll Tearsheet, and their droll, inebriated companions. The idea of a contemporary alehouse in the middle of serious play about English history must have been extraordinarily surprising to his audience—and something with which they could immediately identify. Taverns, pubs, bars, and nightclubs soon became the perfect onstage venues for the resourceful dramatist, from such canonical eighteenth-century British comedies as *The Beaux Stratagem* and *She Stoops to Conquer* (where taverns provide the perfect settings for mistaken identities) to George M. Cohan's 1920 comedy, aptly named *The Tavern*, where mysterious misadventures occur at Freeman's Tavern during an archetypical "dark and stormy night."

NOT THROWING AWAY MY SHOT

Occasionally, the world of Broadway moves from a fictional drinking spot to a real one. Among the world's most legendary taverns would surely be Fraunces Tavern, located in New York City on Pearl Street near Battery Park. A corner office building turned into a tavern called the Queen's Head by Samuel Fraunces in 1762, the site would be key to several important historical gatherings before, during, and after the Revolutionary War.

In the 2015 musical *Hamilton*, its eponymous hero makes his first musical declaration of self at Fraunces Tavern (so designated in the stage directions, but not specifically mentioned in the text). "My Shot" brings five of the musical's protagonists—John Laurens, Hercules Mulligan, Marquis de Lafayette, Aaron Burr, and, of course, Alexander Hamilton—together for an evening of roistering, showboating, and polemicizing, all of which would have been perfectly situated at Fraunces Tavern, a watering hole for commercial organizations and social clubs such as the Chamber of Commerce and the New York Sons of Liberty. Our five musical comrades hoist a tankard or two (or three), professing their thirst for American independence and, as Mulligan puts it, "a Sam Adams or two." (The real Samuel Adams—John Adams's cousin and a firebrand for colonial revolution--ran a malting business outside of Boston.)

But even with malt, beer, or otherwise, the actions of *Hamilton* and its cast of characters bring us to another, far more seminal intoxicant: rum. Rum was the alcoholic beverage that coursed through the veins of Colonial America and its manufacture was the throbbing heartbeat among the islands of the Caribbean. The sugar cane industry, imported to several of the Caribbean islands, most notably Barbados, in the sixteenth century by Spanish, British, and Portuguese entrepreneurs, was essentially the world's first international commercial enterprise; its products were spread all over the globe with enormous economic and cultural implications.

The cane industry's two connected by-products were molasses—a thick, dark-brown sugar concentrate boiled down from sugar cane—and rum, which was distilled from molasses into a powerfully potent brew. Both products were key to the economy of colonial America. By the late 1770s, when *Hamilton* is set, there were dozens of rum distilleries in New England and its denizens drank millions of gallons per year. Several of the historical characters appearing in *Hamilton* have some connection to the rum trade. Hamilton himself was born in Nevis and St. Kitts, a twin-island country in the Caribbean (although not itself a major outpost of the rum industry) and spent some of his early career in New York City working for a firm that managed British tariffs on the importation of rum.

The slave trade was the ghastly engine that energized the commercial mechanism of the rum industry; it became known as the "Triangle

Trade." Essentially, the West Indies sent molasses to the New England colonies so they could distill their own rum; that rum was bought by European traders to purchase enslaved labor from Western Africa; those tormented souls were shipped to the West Indies to work on the vast and unforgiving sugar-cane plantations.

This financial mechanism was highlighted at, of all places, a major climax of *Hamilton*'s founding forbear, *1776*, an unprecedentedly serious musical look at the Declaration of Independence. Opening in 1969, at the height of the Vietnam War, the show was set in Philadelphia in the hot summer leading up to the vote on independence on July 4th. The essential moment toward the musical's climax comes in a barnburner of a solo entitled "Molasses to Rum," when Edward Rutledge, a Congressional delegate from South Carolina, calls out his "Northern brethren" for their hypocrisy regarding slavery—they are eager to condemn it as a practice, but more than willing to propagate it "for the shilling":

> **Whose fortunes are made**
> **In the Triangle Trade?**
> **Hail slavery!**
> **The New England dream.**

The kind of the bibulous comradery celebrated in *Hamilton* isn't present in *1776*—at one point, John Adams asks Benjamin Franklin to join him for dinner and a tankard at the local tavern, but Franklin, wearying of the "obnoxious and disliked" Adams, begs off, citing a date with a comely young thing. *Hamilton* returns several times to various settings of celebrations and public convocations around drink, including "One Last Time," that, although it musicalizes George Washington's farewell to the nation, embraces the sentiment of Washington's 1783 farewell to his troops, which occurred at Fraunces Tavern.

PULL OUT THE STOPPER! LET'S HAVE A WHOPPER!

The British cousin to the tavern—the pub—provides a conducive setting in various musicals; all that tankard banging makes for a nice percussive beat to underscore the obligatory music-hall pastiches sung by inebriated customers. American and British musicals such as *Kean, The Girl Who Came to Supper, Half a Sixpence,* and so on, each feature a standard tankard-banger. The most memorable of these comes from *Oliver!* in the form of the slightly lubricious "Oom-Pah-Pah," sung by Nancy, who is backed by the intoxicated patrons of the Three Cripples Pub. A close second would be Alfred P. Doolittle's all-nighter in the second act of *My Fair Lady*—"I'm Getting Married in the Morning"—sung as he and his entourage stagger out of a pub on the fringes of Covent Garden. In this song, passing out "under the table" is presented not as an embarrassment, but as the desired highlight of an extended evening of buying drinks for the harmonizing crowd.

Although beer, ale, and lager have long been the fundamentals of the pub scene, by the eighteenth century, London had a new contender for the house drink: gin. Local tariffs put a stop to importation of gin from its native Holland into Britain in the 1700s, so metropolitan drinkers turned to their own homemade brews which often used cheap and unspeakable additions to up their potency and questionable taste, including turpentine and sulfuric acid. This led to the so-called "Gin Craze" in London in the eighteenth century, an epidemic of inebriation in lower-class neighborhoods that debilitated entire families within entire swaths of city blocks. By the Victorian era, with the help of the intervention of governmental standards, gin became a better product and was served in a better location, often in a polished and buffed indoor space called a "gin palace," the precursor to the modern bar and suitable for respectable customers with disposable incomes.

QUICK, THOUGH, THE TRADE IS BRISK

If this transition from unspeakable comestibles to respectable consumerism in Victorian England sounds like the opening to the second act of *Sweeney Todd: The Demon Barber of Fleet Street*, that's probably no accident. At the climax of Act One, in Stephen Sondheim and Hugh Wheeler's divinely demonic musical, the eponymous character and his accomplice, Mrs. Lovett, discover how to pass off a most revolting product to the ravenous populace of London. When the curtain comes up—figuratively speaking—after intermission, we see how well their business plan has succeeded. Mrs. Lovett's rundown pie shop now has its own outdoor garden, packed with customers, banging their tankards, demanding more hot pies, and washing them down with ale and gin. An article in *The Illustrated London News of 1848* could have easily served as the stage directions to the second-act opener to *Sweeney Todd*, "God, That's Good!":

> These [establishments] have been transformed from dingy pot-houses into splendid gin-palaces, from painted deal to polished mahogany, from plain useful fittings to costly luxurious adornments. The comfortable old landlady is less seen than formerly, esconced [sic] behind and amongst her rich store of cordials and compounds and liqueurs; she, too, must pass under the hands of the milliner before making her daily appearance in public. Even the pot-boy is not the pot-boy of other days; there is a dash of something about him that may almost be called gentility.

TO US AND OUR GOOD FORTUNE!

A much simpler—and, hopefully, much more wholesome—nineteenth-century tavern is at the center of the little village of Anatevka in the 1964 blockbuster *Fiddler on the Roof*. Reb Mordcha's inn is the setting for a barter based on mistaken identities: the prosperous butcher Lazar Wolf wants to marry the daughter of the impoverished dairyman, Tevye; Tevye thinks that Lazar Wolf wants to buy his milk cow. The Yiddish writer Sholem Aleichem, whose short stories form the basis of *Fiddler*'s plot, wrote about the power of the local tavern: "[It] gave off an irresistible force. It was a magnet, drawing on all the draymen and all the travelers going from one shtetl to the other."

We get an immediate sense of the drinking culture in the shtetl of turn-of-the-century Russia when Lazar Wolf asks Mordcha for a bottle of brandy and two glasses. A moment later, a group of non-Jewish Russians enters and asks for a bottle of vodka: a spirited culture clash. During the scene that follows, the misunderstanding between Tevye and Lazar Wolf resolves itself and there's nothing left to do but toast the making of a match and one another's health and,

ABOVE When a milkman meets a butcher: Zero Mostel as Tevye in *Fiddler on the Roof* (1964) toasts his good fortune with Lazar Wolf at the local tavern in Anatevka.

given Lazar's immediate joy and the depth of his purse, buy a round of drinks for everyone in the tavern, including the Russians. It gives both clans something to think about and something to drink about, celebrating both in Hebrew with "L'Chaim" and in Russian with "Nazdrovia." In this unassuming inn, the bill of fare would have been limited to vodka for the Russian clientele and a simple kind of locally brewed brandy for the Jewish customers, known more popularly as schnapps. As the resulting joyous musical number "L'Chaim" has it:

> We'll raise a glass and sip a drop
>   of schnapps
> In honor of the great good luck
> That favored you.

In this case, and in this Eastern European locality, the schnapps would have been distilled from plums, apricots, or some other combination of fruit—more popularly called slivovitz—and would have been decanted from a keg and brought to the table in a ceramic bottle with a couple of mugs to facilitate its enjoyment.

Drinking alcoholic beverages is not a particular manifestation of Jewish culture. Of course, ceremonial wine is consumed during any number of religious ceremonies, most specifically the Kiddush, a prayer that introduces the Sabbath and requires that at least one glass of wine be drunk. This ritual is used twice in *Fiddler on the Roof*: first, in the Sabbath Prayer sequence, and, later, at the eventual wedding of Tevye's daughter and Motel the tailor, her spouse of choice.

RIGHT A real nightclub or one on stage? The Broadway Theatre seemed to hold both when it hosted Sammy Davis, Jr. (as part of the Will Mastin Trio) in the backstage musical *Mr. Wonderful* (1956). Chita Rivera, right, seems unimpressed with Davis's antics; offstage, it was another story entirely.

(Poor Lazar Wolf.) But drinking is largely confined in Jewish culture to ceremonies and to toasts, rather than private drinking; in fact, it is considered somewhat rude, if not irreligious, to refuse a toast at an engagement, wedding, bar or bat mitzvah, and even a circumcision. Whether or not that adds up to a fair amount of booze on a weekly basis is subject to the kind of Talmudic debate that is best resolved by Anatevka's beloved rabbi.

AND THE BARS ARE PACKED WITH COUPLES CALLING FOR MORE

By the end of *Fiddler on the Roof*, Tevye and his community are forced to leave the shtetl life and emigrate to the four corners of the globe. One of the most famous immigrants from Russia would be Irving Berlin, who arrived in New York in 1893 and promptly moved with his impoverished family to a tenement in Chinatown. Armed with a propensity for singing in public, Berlin found an early job as a singing waiter in a downtown bar called the Pelham Café, where he would belt out popular tunes while serving mugs of beer. It was a prime example of a new American occupation.

The idea that booze and popular ditties were a potent combination for a good time took hold very quickly at the turn of the twentieth century in urban saloons, but once the 1920s came around, even under the restrictive rules of Prohibition, there was the desire for more sophisticated establishments for consenting adults. Hence, the introduction of that rarefied, sophisticated, and all too briefly popular performance and drinking establishment called the nightclub, which traded in sawdust floors for parqueted floors and foaming tankards for cocktail coupes.

Nightclubs—as the name suggests—performed their most compelling work after the sun went down. They were complimentary additions to the theater, to dinner, to the movies—to whatever—and provided an extended evening out on the town, often until the wee small hours.

Manhattan nightclubs such as The Stork Club and El Morocco were so elegant and "in" that they were featured in lyrics by Oscar Hammerstein and Cole Porter and provided a proving ground for emerging entertainers and performers. Small wonder, then, that the nightclub became an ideal setting for a musical comedy; it had everything you could ask for—a sophisticated setting, elegant costumes, and the opportunity to provide a musical number that functioned as, well, a musical number in the context of a performance.

One of the earliest examples of this kind of a performative number was in Jerome Kern and Oscar Hammerstein's *Show Boat* (1927), where Chicago's Trocadero Music Hall is used—both as a rehearsal room and onstage in its nightclub setting—to present two classic songs, "Bill" and a reprise of "Can't Help Lovin' Dat Man." Nightclubs would be deployed ever after in a variety of forms, from a German speakeasy in a rare flop by George and Ira Gershwin called *Pardon My English* (1933) to *The Color Purple* (2005), where a Black juke joint in the South provides a venue for some high-flying numbers. *Mr. Wonderful*, a 1956 musical starring Sammy Davis Jr.—then known mostly for being a nightclub entertainer—takes the concept to its furthest permutation; the second act was pretty much just Davis's nightclub act remounted on a set that depicted—wait for it—a nightclub. Hey—it ran a year, so it must have worked. Anyway, the songs performed in onstage nightclubs are rarely central to the action in the show itself, but often provide excellent opportunities for performers to do their thing and for writers to create one-off numbers that might achieve some popularity outside of the context of the show.

PLANT YOU NOW, DIG YA LATER

Within the various experiments using the night-club setting in Broadway shows, one show stands out in particular. Richard Rodgers and Lorenz Hart's adaptation of John O'Hara's collection of short stories about an intellectually limited and morally neglectful young singer who tries to break into the Chicago nightclub scene during the late-Depression era: *Pal Joey*. Joey Evans is a man of minimal talent, but with an expansive (and expensive) libido, who manages to romance every chorus girl in the nightclub dance line, all while expanding his horizons by seducing a married woman of social standing and economic means named Vera Simpson. *Pal Joey* also offered Rodgers and Hart a canvas on which to portray the most absurd and amusing variations of the kind of second-rate stuff seen in nightclubs in major cities across America. In fact, half the score is based on these kinds of pastiches, employing hyper-caffeinated tenors crooning ridiculous odes to rainbows and flower gardens, while the ladies of the ensemble manage to wiggle and wriggle their way across the stage in various states of undress. The New York audience of 1940 recognized these shenanigans instantly, and because Rodgers and Hart were so skilled at also developing the emotional language of their songwriting material in the offstage sequences, the show reached a level of sophistication—if not critical approbation—far beyond anything seen up to that time.

While the hero of *Pal Joey* doesn't drink much himself, if at all, two of the three ladies most important to the plot certainly do. His married paramour asks the waiter for a Scotch and water, while a nonplussed female reporter asks for a double Scotch and water—"and make it a St. James Scotch, don't try to pass it off with a Jameson's Irish whisky."

Nevertheless, *Pal Joey* demonstrated a particularly sharp eye for all the denizens of nightclubs and their specific drinking patterns and how their habits affect the casual morality of their comings and goings. Because of its neat location to Lake Michigan and its decade-long reputation for crime and bootlegging during Prohibition, Chicago provided an apt and colorful setting for *Pal Joey* and its louche environment. Nightclubs within the Loop and along Michigan Avenue had a storied reputation in the Thirties and beyond. Chief among them was probably the Chez Paree, a vast nightclub with several side rooms and a stage for entertainers as varied and impressive as Sophie Tucker, Jimmy Durante, Edgar Bergen and Charlie McCarthy, and a young trio of singers called the Gumm Sisters, the youngest of whom eventually changed her name to Judy Garland. When the Chez Paree entered the postwar years, a young dancer named Bob Fosse also graced its stages; his off-stage antics not only paralleled those of Joey Evans, but he even played Joey in a New York revival of the musical in the 1960s.

Act One of *Pal Joey* ends with a dream ballet—yes, a dream ballet that predates by three years *Oklahoma!*—in which Joey imagines his own sublime nightclub called Chez Joey, with all the concomitant elements of sophisticated café society, such as a bedecked clientele of countesses and ambassadors quaffing expensive Champagne and being photographed for the society column.

COME BLOW YOUR HORN, START CELEBRATING

And, yet, Joey Evans could not possibly have dreamed of the exotic and extravagant characteristics of Berlin's Kit Kat Klub—easily the most famous nightclub in musical theater history. The cabaret began life as an underground club called The Lady Windermere in the pages of Christopher Isherwood's 1939 novella *Welcome to Berlin*, an account based on his own experiences as a young expatriate writer in Weimar Germany during the rise of the Third Reich. The uncomfortable charm of what became the Kit Kat Klub was part and parcel of Berlin's nightclub scene in

the 1920s, an era of decadence unrivaled in modern drinking history. Between the wars, free of America's puritanical Prohibition, Berlin became the epicenter for social entertainment—reports confirm that in 1930 there were 899 licensed cabarets and nightclubs that permitted dancing; one can only imagine the innumerable rathskellers, underground clubs, and holes-in-the-wall that did not bother to obtain a license.

The musical *Cabaret*, derived from Isherwood's stories, was not only set primarily in the Kit Kat Klub, but the Kit Kat Klub also gave the show its musical vocabulary. *Cabaret* probably uses performative songs more successfully than any other musical, as its creators cleverly contrasted the musical numbers performed by the Emcee and the low-rent chanteuse Sally Bowles in the Kit Kat Klub with a subtle way of advancing their larger narrative—the corrupting and corrosive rise of the Third Reich among the citizens of Berlin. The cabaret itself is less memorable perhaps than the performers who graced its postage-stamp-sized stages, but we do get a sense of the idiosyncratic elements of a Berlin nightclub, including its buffet of sexual preferences and the way in which customers could flirt with one another via private telephones installed at their tables. (Actual Berlin nightclubs even had pneumatic tubes connecting tables so patrons could pass private notes.) The zeitgeist of *Cabaret* is so deeply tied to its venue that it hardly came as a surprise when the extremely successful revival of the late 1990s eventually moved into the space that once held Studio 54—the most infamous nightclub of its era, the 1970s.

Actual drinking in *Cabaret* is certainly suggested among the Kit Kat Klub's many patrons, but it's not given any particular overt presentation in the plot. The only real meaningful moments of imbibing are given to Herr Schultz, the Jewish shopkeeper, who gets a little tipsy on schnapps during his engagement party. This leads to several indiscreet comments in front of

his guests, one of whom is a member of the Nazi Party. Our heroine, Sally Bowles, is certainly not a Temperance leader, but her major contribution to drinking is not with a cocktail but with a hangover remedy called the prairie oyster: raw eggs swooshed up in a toothbrush glass with a shot of Worcestershire sauce. Whether that works or not is entirely a matter of conjecture, but Sally also gives us a toast worthy of a L'Chaim or two: "Hals- und Beinbruch," which is German for "neck and leg break."

"It's supposed to stop it from happening," she says optimistically.

I KNEW MY MORALE WOULD CRACK

One would think that a musical set in Times Square, with two nightclub numbers and a bevy of gamblers and sinners should inspire a veritable battalion of boozehounds, but in 1950's *Guys and Dolls*, the biggest boozer happens to be a Mission doll. As part of the intricate (and very satisfying) plot of the Frank Loesser musical, Sarah Brown, the punctilious leader of the Salvation Army mission, Broadway chapter, allows herself to be brought on a dinner date to Havana, Cuba, by gambler extraordinaire Sky Masterson. After visiting various tourist spots, they arrive at the Hotel Nacional de Cuba (also the site for major plot points in *The Godfather, Part II*, by the way), and Sky decides it's time for a round of drinks—two "Dulce de Leche"s, in coconut shells, no less. Sarah, who's spanking new to this kind of international bar-hopping, asks what's in a "Dulce de Leche." "Oh, sugar," says Sky, "and—sort of a native flavoring. Bacardi."

As the evening wears on, Sarah has more than a few Dulce de Leches—"a great way to get children to drink their milk," she avers—and winds up shedding her puritanical demeanor, singing the great ballad, "If I Were a Bell"—a classic take on the shopworn trope of the prim gal who lets her pinned-up hair down after being introduced to a cocktail.

Very sound musical comedy dramaturgy—except there's no such thing as a Dulce de Leche cocktail. Although Bacardi is obviously the major rum distiller of Cuba (and quite a few drinks fit quite comfortably in coconut shells), that where the accuracy ends. Dulce de Leche is instead a thick caramel sauce served over ice cream. Perhaps bookwriter Abe Burrows was thinking more of a *coquito*, a Puerto Rican rum-based eggnog (also a great way to get kids to drink their milk). Ironic that among all the denizens of loose morality in *Guys and Dolls* (including Nicely-Nicely Johnson, who, in "Sit Down, You're Rocking the Boat," only dreams of a whiskey bottle in his fist), it's Sarah Brown who greets the street-washed dawn of Times Square with a hell of a hangover.

No doubt, at the crack of dawn, Sarah and Sky would have encountered an inebriate or two staggering out of some Irish bar or seedy gin mill in midtown. In New York City, from the Depression through World War II and into the 1950s, that carouser would have almost always been uniquely male; patrons of drink emporiums were a coterie of a brotherhood—women were not terribly welcome at the neighborhood bar, and an unescorted, unmarried woman sitting at a bar betokened something else entirely.

WHERE CAN YOU TAKE A GIRL?

But by the end of the 1960s, gender stereotypes and restrictions had loosened up considerably, and if any musical of the period kept the drinks flowing for men *and* women, it was 1968's *Promises, Promises*—one of, if not *the*, booziest musicals ever to stumble onto Broadway.

Based on Billy Wilder's Academy Award-winning 1960 film *The Apartment*, *Promises, Promises* ups the movie's ante by having another decade under its belt and using this update to land itself smack-dab in the Swinging Sixties, ably abetted by a first-rate score by two of the most reliable

LEFT Yes, yes—we know it's the film version of *Guys and Dolls*. But who could resist all those coconut shell drinks? By the way, that's Marlon Brando as Sky Masterson and Jean Simmons as Sister Sarah Brown, ringing each other's bells.

songwriters of the decade, Burt Bacharach and Hal David. Memorializing the *Mad Men*-era forty years before it became a television phenomenon (and cliché), the musical is centered around the extramarital affairs conducted by account executives high up in a (presumably) Sixth Avenue insurance corporation and a poor schmuck named C. C. Baxter whom the executives inveigle to lend his apartment for their quickie trysts, all of which seem to be highly lubricated by some form of alcohol. The bottle count in *Promises, Promises* must have taxed even the most even-tempered props master—innumerable glasses of beer, Champagne, vodka, sherry, scotch, even a bottle of Tom and Jerry mix, a kind of eggnog additive that used to be quite popular around Christmas. Baxter's neighbor, believing that he, rather than the executive joy boys, is responsible for such intemperate high jinks remarks: "The garbage man tells me the only place he picks up more empty bottles is the Copacabana."

The bacchanalias in *Promises, Promises* extend to an office Christmas party, where Baxter observes that a necking couple must be really drunk because "those two are married to each other," and onward to include not one, not two, not three, but *four* separate bar scenes. The first of these is the hero's favorite bar on Second Avenue, with the punningly conceived (by book writer Neil Simon) name of the Grapes of Roth. As Baxter tells the audience, "It could be any bar on Second Avenue . . . Your Mother's Hairnet, The Booze Boutique, Helen's Navel . . . , As a matter of fact, my favorite Second Avenue bar is on First Avenue." If this all sounds effortfully comic to a twenty-first-century listener, the patter was actually rather authentic about a drinking phenomenon of the late 1960s (and one that didn't exist when Wilder made his original film in 1960): the singles bar.

New York's Upper East Side had fairly cheap real estate in the 1960s and became an affordable neighborhood for single working men and women. In 1965, one entrepreneur realized there might be interest in a different kind of bar scene—besides the darkened, male-oriented Irish bars of midtown—that would entice a new generation of drinkers. TGI Fridays opened at First Avenue and 63rd Street with a fresh décor (ferns, Tiffany lamps) and a playful cocktail list (with offerings such as Harvey Wallbangers—a not-so-subtle clue to the sexual side of the bar's appeal). Apparently, its founder knew that, for some reason, dozens of stewardesses lived on the block; at any rate, there was certainly a large number of single women who wanted to go out and enjoy themselves without the silent censoriousness of the midtown, male-dominated bar scene. Within a year or two, the Upper East Side was known as New York's "swingiest square mile" and soon 85 bars sprung up, each with names that threatened to the other in conspicuous "hipness": Maxwell's Plum, Mister Laff's, Adam's Apple, Daly's Daffodil. Neil Simon wasn't just satirizing the singles bar scene—he was practically a documentarian.

The most essential bar scene in *Promises, Promises* comes—as well it should, for maximum poignancy—on Christmas Eve at Clancy's Lounge "a seedy bar on Eighth Avenue." It's here that Baxter, nursing a broken heart, finds himself "cheaping up slosh whiskey . . . slopping up cheap whiskey." He meets a widow (at least that's what she claims) named Marge McDougall, an attractive sport with a taste for double vodka stingers. Several rounds later, Baxter and Marge are comfortable enough with each other to leave the bar and return to his apartment together—but not before being sent on their way with a chorus number at the bar sung and danced by its Yuletide patrons, who carouse merrily and intoxicatedly about the New Year around the bend, encouraging each other to "forget the past and think about the present."

A sentiment that perfectly tops up the American musical's romance with ballads, bars, and booze.

THE HAMILTON SHOT

(Inspired by *Hamilton*, 2015)

There's no way to have a *Hamilton* cocktail without making it a "shot"—and there's also no way to have a *Hamilton* cocktail without basing it on rum.

Alexander Hamilton was born in the Caribbean nation of Saint Kitts and Nevis; the rum imported from there comes only in flavored varieties. Luckily, the Ministry of Rum on the isle of Guyana produces a label called—wait for it—Hamilton Rum, and their New York Blend is both apposite and potent.

However, rum—or most commercially available rums—isn't often quaffed as a shot, so this cocktail is a way of honoring the tradition of the show while creating a palatable drink.

LOWBALL OR OLD-FASHIONED*

Demerara sugar

1 ounce dark coffee liqueur, such as Mr. Black (no cream additive)

2 ounces Hamilton rum

Rim the edge of the glass by wetting the lip and dipping it in Demerara sugar.
Pour the coffee liqueur into the bottom of the glass. Add one large ice cube.
Pour the rum slowly over the ingredients. Stir gently with a bar spoon
(so as not to dislodge the sugar from the rim of the glass) or even swirl in your
hand as if you were a big shot; let sit for a moment to chill the ingredients.
Then retire to a room where it happens, and bottoms up!

— WHAT IS DEMERARA SUGAR? —

Demerara sugar comes directly from the sugar cane of the West Indies. The crystals are amber-colored and crunchy, so you might want to grind them down a bit. This unusual sugar can be found in most grocery stores (Domino produces several varieties).

* SOMETHING HEAVY THAT FITS IN YOUR HAND LIKE A TUMBLER

THE L'CHAIM

(Inspired by *Fiddler on the Roof*, 1964)

A sophisticated cocktail seems incompatible with an impoverished Russian shtetl. On the other hand—why not? There are certainly enough appropriate ingredients suggested by the text to create a miracle of miracles.

The main spirit in the L'Chaim is schnapps, in this case the most readily available schnapps in the States, slivovitz, a brandy derived from plums. Given that our hero, Tevye, is a dairyman, some heavy cream would make for an essential addition. Freshly ground nutmeg adds an earthy and traditional dimension to the cocktail.

If the L'Chaim resembles a Brandy Alexander, that's not unintentional; the czar of Russia at the turn of the century was Alexander III (as in "May God bless and keep the czar—far away from us!"). He was particularly antagonistic to the Jews and initiated the pogroms that drove the residents of Anatevka from their homes. So, it's a bit of poetic justice to repossess the ingredients of his namesake cocktail.

If you want to have a truly *Fiddler* experience, bring along a bottle of Russian vodka—Stolichanaya would do nicely—and toast yourself (or some other tavern dwellers) in between L'Chaim cocktails.

COUPE
+ COCKTAIL SHAKER

1 ounce slivovitz
1 ounce crème de cacao (Tempus Fugit or Giffard; go for the good—and clear—stuff)

1 ounce heavy cream
1 whole nutmeg seed (about the size of an olive)

Pour the slivovitz, crème de cacao, and heavy cream into a cocktail shaker. Add ice, shake well, then strain into a coupe. You could be historically more accurate and serve the drink in a ceramic mug, but you'd be missing out on the swell look of this cocktail. Use a fine grater or a mortar and pestle to unleash the fresh nutmeg and sprinkle a few nutmeg shavings over the top of the drink. That's what the folks in Anatevka would do.

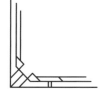

THE BLOODY SWEENEY

(Inspired by *Sweeney Todd: The Demon Barber of Fleet Street*, 1978)

Among the freely flowing liquids of *Sweeney Todd*, gin comes in a close second.

The devious Mrs. Lovett uses a "tot of gin" to lull the young Toby into a state of contented compliance, while Sweeney dispatches with Toby's employer in his upstairs barber shop. And gin becomes a reliable complementary beverage to the unreliable meat pies eventually served by Mrs. Lovett.

But, clearly, gin can't really compete in *Sweeney Todd*, so you have to go to a bloody good cocktail—inevitably, the Bloody Mary. This is a derivation of a derivation known as a Red Snapper, and it uses gin, as any good cocktail based on a musical set in Victorian England must. Now, I'd suggest using an old-fashioned British gin such as Gordon's or Plymouth (both of which were around in Sweeney's time) and, for the seasoning, a generous pinch of Old Bay seasoning. Why? You may remember that Sweeney returns to London at the top of the musical after having been transported to Botany Bay on a trumped-up charge; so that'll do. Now, if you're a proper artist with a knife, you might amuse your guests by trimming and shaping a robust celery stalk into the shape of a razor and adding it to the garnish.

Readers, it's really too good at least.

HIGHBALL OR TALL GLASS

3½ ounces tomato juice (Sacramento will do nicely)

1½ ounces gin

2 tablespoons Worcestershire sauce

2 tablespoons lime juice

1 generous pinch Old Bay seasoning

½ teaspoon horseradish (optional)

Stalk of celery (or a firm slice of cucumber), to garnish

Pour all the ingredients (minus garnish) into a mixing glass and add several cubes of ice. Stir gently with a mixing spoon. Transfer to a tall glass, add ice, and garnish appropriately (or even inappropriately). When you move on to your second one, you might want to serve it in a pewter tankard and bang the table while yelling, "More hot pies!"

THE BEWITCHED, BOTHERED, AND BEWILDERED

(Inspired by *Pal Joey*, 1940)

With this cocktail, you can be wild at last and beguiled at last. You can even shorten the name to the Bewitched, which is how disc jockeys, record executives, and cabaret singers have shortened the name of this eternally popular standard from the show.

In the show itself, the ladies—or "mice," as Joey rather impoliticly refers to them—do most of the drinking. To be honest, though, their drinks aren't that interesting. Try this instead. The use of Cognac takes its inspiration from the show's leading lady, Vera Simpson. A "V.S." designation in a Cognac stands for "Very Special," meaning the youngest Cognac in the blend must be a minimum of two years old. (There's also "V.S.O.P."—Very Special Old Pale—which designates a minimum of four years.) It was an unconfirmed rumor that the character of Vera Simpson was named in deference to the actress who originally played her, Vivienne Segal, a particular favorite performer of Rodgers and Hart's; she also portrayed Vera in the fabled 1952 revival, which was more successful than the original run.

The addition of B&B should seem obvious to the Hart-minded wordsmiths out there: the commercial nickname for Brandy and Bénédictine, it contains two of out three letters of the drink's name.

MARTINI
+ COCKTAIL SHAKER

1½ ounces Cognac (or Armagnac, if you like)
1½ ounces B&B
1 orange peel

Pour the two liqueurs into a cocktail shaker. Add ice and shake.
Gently rub the orange peel around the rim of the glass.
Drop into the glass and strain the liqueurs. Plant you now, dig you later!

THE TOAST OF MAYFAIR

(Inspired by *Cabaret*, 1966)

Ladies and gentlemen, *Mesdames et Messieurs, Meine Damen und Herren,* I give you a cocktail inspired by the intoxicating star of the Kit Kat Klub, the toast of Mayfair, Fraulein Sally Bowles.

Sally is rather like a cocktail herself, mixed and composed of several diverse ingredients and influences. She is based on a real cabaret singer named Jean Ross, and writer Christopher Isherwood purloined Sally's surname from his pal, Paul Bowles. Isherwood's Sally purports to be the wayward daughter of a British industrialist: by day, she's a film extra; by night, she sings in a cabaret. The 1972 film version of *Cabaret* complicated Sally's provenance further by making her American to accommodate Liza Minnelli (while changing the show's hero, Cliff, an American, into a British writer). Who cares? So what?

This cocktail, based on the Emcee's introduction of Sally at the bandstand, is inspired by another cocktail that has, sadly perhaps, faded from view: the Mary Pickford. Mary Pickford is exactly the kind of female movie star Sally would have admired in the 1920s, so there it is.

Oddly enough, the addition of pineapple juice—so apposite for Herr Schultz and Frau Schneider, who sing "The Pineapple Song"—was already in the Mary Pickford, so, put down the knitting, the books, and the broom and enjoy.

COUPE

2 ounces British gin

1½ ounces freshly squeezed pineapple juice

1 teaspoon grenadine syrup

1 teaspoon Luxardo maraschino liqueur

½ ounce float sparkling wine

Luxardo maraschino cherry (Optional)

Pomegranate sugar

Rim the edge of the glass by wetting the lip and dipping it in the pomegranate sugar.
Fill the cocktail shaker with ice. Pour the gin, pineapple juice, grenadine,
and Luxardo over the ice; shake, then strain into a coupe. Drizzle the top with
a float of sparkling wine (cava or prosecco); gently add the cherry.

THE LUCKY LADY
AND THE BELLRINGER

(Inspired by *Guys and Dolls*, 1950)

Guess what's in the *Daily News*? Not one, but two cocktails from the world of this classic musical: one for a guy and one for a doll.

What other drink could you come up with to honor this show than a Manhattan? In this case, the Lucky Lady has a bit of a, um, twist: it uses a particular brand of amaro from South Carolina called Southern Amaro Liqueur, manufactured by High Wire Distillery, instead of sweet vermouth. I picked Southern Amaro because I not only appreciate its subtle clove-infused taste, but I also really love its label, which depicts a doll and a riverboat gambler.

As noted earlier, the Dulce de Leche isn't really a drink, so the Bellringer is based on a variation of its theme: Bacardi, of course, some milk products, and plenty of coconut. After a couple of these, you'll go ding-dong-ding-dong-ding!

THE LUCKY LADY

MARTINI
+ COCKTAIL SHAKER

2 ounces rye

1 ounce High Wire Southern Amaro

Dash orange bitters

Lemon peel, to garnish

Fill the cocktail shaker with ice. Pour the rye and amaro over the ice. Shake vigorously, then drain into a martini glass. Twist the lemon peel to release its oil and toss—gently!—into your drink.

THE BELLRINGER

COPPER MUG
(OR MARTINI)
+ COCKTAIL SHAKER

2 ounces white Bacardi rum

1 ounce Clément coconut liqueur

½ ounce evaporated milk

½ ounce cream of coconut (Coco Loco is best)

½ ounce condensed milk

1 cinnamon stick, to garnish

Fill the cocktail shaker with ice. Pour all the liquid ingredients over the ice. Shake vigorously and for a good while (until the condensed milk has broken down). Pour the mixture into a mug or martini glass (unless you have a hollowed-out coconut handy). Garnish with a cinnamon stick, which you can use, demurely, as a straw.

THE TURKEY LURKEY

(Inspired by *Promises, Promises*, 1968)

If one were to be strictly accurate, the *Promises, Promises* cocktail would be a vodka stinger, based on the drink ordered several times by Marge McDougall, the Christmas Eve date of our hero, C. C. Baxter. But, alas, for poor Marge, that cocktail is the sole domain of another Upper East Side lady who lunches, Joanne from *Company*. In the meantime, the consolation for dear Marge was a Tony Award for Best Supporting Actress in a Musical; each of the two times the show appeared on Broadway, the actress playing Marge won a Tony, despite just fourteen minutes of stage time: Marian Mercer in 1969 and Katie Finneran in 2008.

Yuletide cocktails are part and parcel of how and when we enjoy our liquor; certainly, the holidays make us merry and bright. The Turkey Lurkey takes its name from the astonishingly vigorous dance number toward the end of Act One, performed for no good reason at all by three secretaries during an office party. Thankfully, the number choreographed by Michael Bennett can be found on YouTube.

In fact, you might put these ingredients in a cocktail shaker and dance to "Turkey Lurkey Time": if your back holds out, you'll have a hell of a cocktail.

MARTINI
OR COUPE

2 ounces Wild Turkey bourbon

1 ounce crème de menthe (white; Tempus Fugit is an excellent brand)

1 ounce Quaranta y Tres

½ ounce heavy cream

1 peppermint stick or candy cane, to garnish

Pour the bourbon, crème de menthe, Quaranta y Tres, and heavy cream into a cocktail shaker. Add ice. Shake well, then strain the drink into the glass. Slip in a peppermint stick for garnish. Who knows what the future will bring? After a couple of these, a rocky morning, that's for sure!

CHAPTER 6

Show Queens

HERE'S TO
THE LADIES

◇

Entertaining vodka drinkers
Is a job they give to me.
Making nice guys out of stinkers
Seems to be my cup of tea.
—"The Hostess with the Mostes' on the Ball," *Call Me Madam*

I t's one of the most popular and perennial tropes in the American musical: the leading lady enters upstage, center, (and preferably at the top of a staircase), while bedazzled and bedecked members of the chorus toast her by hoisting glasses of Champagne in her general direction, enthralled simply to be in the same room as such a glamorous and captivating lady.

A guy in the same role—hmm, not so much.

But, on Broadway, there seems to be a felicitous match between a star female performer and a round of drinks for everybody in the house (the onstage house, that is). It may be a holdover from the golden age of the operetta, as far back as 1914, when the eponymous merry widow in Franz Lehár's operetta confection, Hanna Glawari, is welcomed into an embassy ballroom by the most well-heeled suitors in all of Paris. This kind of ebullient musical entrance evolved into a time-honored tradition, still the best and most gracious way to welcome a superstar to the proceedings. By the time the Irving Berlin musical *Call Me Madam* reached Broadway in 1950, Ethel Merman was such a huge star—and the proceedings in the plot so accommodating—that she was given three such moments in the show. Twenty years later, when she returned to Broadway and took on the role of Dolly Gallagher Levi in *Hello, Dolly!* (after having turned it down several times during its inception), she finally got to descend the most venerated staircase in musical theater history, serenaded by a chorus of enamored, red-vested waiters. But even the enthusiasm of those waiters paled before the genuflecting chorus members who greeted Lauren Bacall's celebrity avatar Margo Channing when she arrived at a Greenwich Village gay bar in 1970's *Applause*, a scene of obeisance unsurpassed in musical comedy history (and the first appearance of a gay bar in a Broadway musical).

GET THE ICE OUT!

Although Jerry Herman's *Hello, Dolly!* may well be the best-known of these celebratory tropes, it was his next musical, *Mame,* that has endeared itself to Champagne hoisters everywhere. *Mame* was based on a play from a decade earlier, *Auntie Mame* (itself based on an "irreverent escapade" by Patrick Dennis), which was already a musical without music. Spanning a generation from the Roaring

PREVIOUS SPREAD We think she's just sensational: Angela Lansbury makes one of Broadway's grandest entrances in *Mame* (1966).
RIGHT She's partly Jane Fonda, partly Jane Austen—and all *star:* Lauren Bacall in *Applause* (1970).

Twenties to post-World War II, *Mame* focuses on the free-wheeling, gate-crashing, boundaries-bashing peregrinations of Mame Dennis, an irrepressible darling of Manhattan society who manages to surmount any crisis, personal or professional, with the kind of iconoclastic optimism only found in musicals. Given the lead character's propensity for throwing parties and celebrations on a massive scale with only the most meager of motivations, it's not surprising that *Mame* sports one of the highest bottle counts of any Broadway show.

Mame herself is revealed at the height (literally—the obligatory staircase) of a full-fledged affair in her Beekman Place apartment, filled with the leading literary, artistic, and theatrical lights of the Jazz Age. Drinks are flowing, and she declares it a holiday: "One I just invented. The moon's full. The gin's in the bathtub." She proceeds to lead an opening number—"It's Today!"—that's a virtual battle plan for a cocktail party: ice is gotten out, punch bowls are filled, doubles are ordered, Scotch is poured out. . . . By the end of the scene, Mame has also ordered a martini and, the next day, hung over, she orders "a light breakfast": black coffee and a sidecar.

Lest one think Mame is the most hopeless inebriate ever featured in a conventional musical, fear not, as she only comes in second. For contrast—and for some unsentimental laughs—the story also brings in operetta star Vera Charles, Mame's fair-weather bosom buddy, coronated as "the world's greatest lush." Vera is so blotto most of the time that she can't tell the sun from the moon—"My God, it's bright!"—and wakes up in the middle of the day, muttering, "Somebody's been sleeping in my clothes." When she and Mame both swear off booze in the second act, they concur that it's such a good idea, it's worth drinking to it.

Still, Mame's greatest triumph is down South at Peckerwood, a plantation "down Georgia-way," where she charms several generations of elite Southerners, all bluegrass and bluebloods. After her beau "sloshes" another gallon of bourbon into

the communal punch bowl, it gives Mame the fortitude to brave a fox hunt. Although she's never ridden a horse before, she brings the fox back alive, cuddled in her arms. For this, she receives what appears to be the adulation of the entire crowd, complete with all the requisite name-invoking and drink-hoisting: everyone agrees—she's just sensational. And the curtain falls on Act One.

Whatever triumph Mame Dennis had at Peckerwood was nothing compared to the reception accorded to Angela Lansbury when she assumed the mantel of Mame in the original 1966 production. For Lansbury, it was one of the most mature Cinderella stories in Broadway history—becoming the belle of the Broadway ball at the age of forty, an over-the-title success after decades of supporting roles in Hollywood. One of those roles, nearly twenty years earlier, was also one of her best: Kay Thorndyke, the utterly unsentimental heiress to a national newspaper syndicate in Frank Capra's 1948 screen adaptation of the political comedy *State of the Union*.

OPPOSITE When to fold 'em and when to hold 'em: In the 1945 *State of the Union*, Ruth Hussey (left) is no match for Maidel Turner, the New Orleans socialite Lulubelle Alexander.

ABOVE For decades, the musical *Mame* provided guaranteed employment for ladies of a certain age. Here, in a 1970 summer stock production, Elaine Stritch as boozin' buddy Vera Charles shares the stage (I use the term loosely) with Janis Paige as Mame.

I'D RATHER BE TIGHT

The 1945 play *State of the Union* was the kind of utterly worthy but lighthearted stage comedy that would eventually be subsumed by the movies and then by television—indeed, the recent innovation of television itself makes a pioneering cameo appearance in Frank Capra's film version, which starred Spencer Tracy and Katharine Hepburn. But for a postwar Broadway audience, Howard Lindsay and Russel Crouse's play was an eye-opening look into the backroom machinations of the American political system. The lead character, Grant Matthews, is a straight-talking industrialist put forward as a possible candidate for president on the Republican ticket. Backed by a cohort of self-serving operators led by publisher Kay Thorndyke, he's pushed to make a big national speech, following a cocktail party held for half-a-dozen political nabobs in his New York apartment.

The party itself is one of the most jaw-dropping displays of cocktail consumption ever staged in a straight play. (The property list for the play contains twenty-seven cocktails required to perform the twenty-minute scene.) Each of the characters has at least two cocktails, except for a big-time union representative, who stays sober on Coca-Cola, mostly so he can watch everyone else's missteps. The hired bartender keeps whipping up martinis, bourbon-and-water highballs, and one particular cocktail meticulously concocted to keep the wife of a Louisiana judge properly lubricated: the Sazerac, or "Sazarac," as it's spelled in the text.

A Sazerac was such a rarity in the North that its recipe has to be spelled out to the bartender at the cocktail party. But it's a life raft to Lulubelle Alexander, played in both the play and movie by veteran actress Maidel Turner, whose career started in the silent film era. Lulubelle steals the show with her portrayal of genial, jovial inebriation, sending her bloviating husband back to the bar to mix her

another Sazerac whenever he starts another long-winded speech: "Mix the drinks before you start talkin', Jeff—you know how I hate to interrupt you." Lulubelle admits she doesn't even really know what's in a Sazerac, but, after about four of them, she proclaims she hasn't enjoyed herself this much "since Huey Long died." She even manages to get Grant Matthews' wife, Mary, hooked on the cocktail, which becomes momentarily disastrous for the plot and Matthew' own political chances, but not before a thoroughly potted Mary gets off a great one-liner: "I'd rather be tight than be president."

Mary gets drunk, of course, to everyone's consternation, but it only leads her to a higher consciousness—*in vino veritas*—a predicament played out in numerous shows, such as *The Philadelphia Story* and Cole Porter's adaptation of *Ninotchka*, *Silk Stockings*. The prevailing notion—morally and dramatically—is that good girls and alcohol don't mix.

COULD SOMEONE PINCH ME, PLEASE?

If that was the case, you certainly wouldn't want to celebrate a good *little* girl with alcohol. The pint-sized star of *Annie* gets celebrated by an enthusiastic chorus of employees several times in her eponymous musical, originally with such songs as "I Think I'm Gonna Like It Here" and "Annie" (rewritten for the 1982 film as "We Got Annie"), although none of the various maids, butlers, and other factotums at the Warbucks estate would ever think of raising a glass of booze in her honor.

Which is somewhat ironic, as the original character of "Little Orphan Annie," who first appeared in Harold Gray's comic strip back in 1924, became celebrated by an entire generation for her connection to a different kind of beverage: a barley-based powdered milk supplement called Ovaltine. Ovaltine was the commercial sponsor for Annie's first foray into showbiz, a radio show broadcast out of Chicago in 1930, then promptly

OPPOSITE Staircases aren't just for mature leading ladies; here Lilla Crawford as *Annie* in the 2012 revival thinks she's gonna like it there.

picked up for coast-to-coast broadcast by NBC. To say that Ovaltine used the relatively new medium of radio to promote its product would be an understatement; youngsters across the country were practically indoctrinated by the program to purchase the stuff. Kids were asked to mail in the aluminum seal inside of each jar of Ovaltine to become members of Annie's Secret Society and receive a special decoder ring that allowed them to decipher secret messages broadcast on the program itself—fans of *A Christmas Story* will remember how prepubescent listeners could become obsessed with the promotion. The product itself was less compelling; the company also promoted an Annie-embossed shake-up mug, but, practically speaking, to get the stuff to dissolve in milk, you needed a cement mixer.

Still, the idea of kids having a drink of their own, even before Prohibition ended, was a potent one (relatively speaking). By the mid-1930s, Little Orphan Annie was given a run for her money as America's most beloved, unflappable moppet by movie star Shirley Temple. It wasn't long before Temple got her own signature beverage as well: the Shirley Temple. This concoction wasn't the brainchild of an advertising executive or public relations flack at Fox. Its origin is lost in the mists of anecdote. However, it was most probably originated by a clever bartender in Hollywood. Temple herself thought it was created by a bartender at the Brown Derby who mixed ginger ale and grenadine syrup and topped it off with a maraschino cherry. She wasn't a fan: "Too sweet," she once said in a 1986 interview with NPR, "I hated them."

It's unlikely the no-nonsense Annie Warbucks would have tolerated them either although surely it would have been preferable to the bathtub gin swilled by the warden of her orphanage, Miss Hannigan.

WOULD YOU PULL THAT STUFF WITH ANNETTE?

That contrast between being a "good girl" who doesn't drink and a "bad girl" who does is a major plot point in *Grease*. Written in 1972—only a scant pseudo-generation from the mid-Fifties it celebrates so raucously—it was an early marker of the nostalgia craze of the Seventies and its version of the high-school zeitgeist during the Eisenhower years was viewed without rose-colored glasses, cat-eye or otherwise. In fact, the original Broadway show—before it was co-opted by Hollywood, numerous cut-and-paste revivals, and a zillion high-school productions—was quite frank in its exploration of teenaged rituals, such as ratting your hair, getting pinned, smoking "ciggie-butts," losing your virginity, and raiding your parents' liquor cabinet.

Crossing the territory between "good" (i.e., uncool) and "bad" (i.e., accepted into the informal fraternities and sororities of Rydell High—the Burger Palace Boys and the Pink Ladies) is really the entire plot of *Grease*. Not surprisingly, booze features significantly in that trajectory. Nice girl Sandra Dumbrowsky, who moves to town at the start of the school year, is forced to run the gauntlet one night during a pajama party at the home of Marty, a lieutenant in the Pink Ladies. Sandy's lack of cool is robustly mocked by Betty Rizzo, the gang's leader and self-proclaimed arbiter of lunchroom hauteur: "You gotta get with it! Otherwise, forget about it! Go back to your hot cocoa and Girl Scout cookies!" What self-respecting high-schooler could refuse that challenge? In sequential order, Sandy inhales her first cigarette, swigs from a proffered half-gallon jug of Italian Swiss Colony ("Wow, it's imported!" squeals one Pink Lady), and gets her ears pierced rather crudely, with a sewing needle. Of course, she winds up tossing her cookies in the bathroom (from the piercing—not the wine).

As much as *Grease* is about growing up, the original was quite canny about not showing any actual grown-ups, or more accurately, any parents (there is a schoolteacher or two). In this, it mirrors another avatar of popular culture, also created in the 1950s, *Peanuts*, which also realized that when focusing on kids the last thing one wants to see is a grown-up. While Sandy was getting indoctrinated into cool-hood upstairs at her friend's house, it's not impossible that the grown-ups were downstairs having a cocktail party in the living room or "rec room," roistering around the brand-new hi-fi set, digging hors d'oeuvres to the latest easy-listening tunes "conducted" by Jackie Gleason. Before World War II, around 30 percent of social drinking was done at home, while the remainder was done publicly in bars and restaurants; in the 1950s, that ratio was reversed—the living room cocktail party became a social phenomenon. That phenomenon also ushered in a round of cocktails that, liberated from the corner saloon, became institutions for middle-class consumption: Vodka Collins, White Russians, Whiskey Sours, Seven & Sevens, Brandy Alexanders, and more. A bunch of high-school seniors in their p.j.s upstairs chugging Thunderbird seems a lot less cool by comparison. Still, cool is in the eye of the beholder, and when the transformed Sandy Dubrowski makes her final appearance in *Grease*, French-inhaling cigarettes, clad in skin-tight pants, she has finally joined the ranks of the Pink Ladies. ("She actually looks prettier and more alive than she ever has," reads the stage direction.). Sandy is a good girl who now looks *great*.

WOULDN'T IT BE LOVERLY?

"I'm a good girl, I am," avers Eliza Doolittle in the first act of *My Fair Lady*. Her desire for creature comforts is pretty simple and spelled out quite clearly in her first number: it includes one

enormous chair, someone's head resting on her knee, and lots of chocolate. Liquor doesn't seem to enter into it at all. This is in direct contrast to Eliza's father, who wants to spend every spare farthing he has on himself and his mates at the pub—or, for that matter, to her aunt (mentioned in the Ascot scene), for whom gin is mother's milk. In the Edwardian world in which Eliza is learning to spread her wings, alcohol can be a precise dividing line between respectability and disgrace, and she is quite keen on not crossing that line.

Still, *My Fair Lady* is predicated on Eliza transforming into, if not a duchess, at least a Mame. The end of the first act at the Embassy Ball is her proverbial "walk down the staircase," everyone "ooh-ing" and "aah-ing" and wondering about her identity. All the scene lacks is that fully bedecked chorus, hoisting their glasses in hosannas and praising her glorious triumph. Of course, that *does* happen in *My Fair Lady*—just not to Eliza, but to Professor Higgins at the beginning of Act Two. Eliza has, alas, to be content with passing herself off as a prospective consort to some hypothetical head of state.

JUST A LITTLE TOUCH OF STAR QUALITY

Of course, if the lady's preoccupation is in becoming an *actual* head of state, there's *Evita*. Tim Rice and Andrew Lloyd Webber's 1979 musical epic of Eva Peròn's ascent and descent as First Lady and power broker of post-World War II Argentina boasts a cornucopia of bad behavior: serial infidelity, financial corruption, authoritarian oppression—that kind of thing. Eva Peròn becomes the kind of "bad girl" that Betty Rizzo could only dream of in her most Thunderbird-infused imaginings. As Evita admits herself, when she's still Eva Duarte, dreaming of hitting it big in Buenos Aires: "I'm so bad, I'm good." Later, when Eva is considering abetting Juan Peron in taking over the country, Peròn posits another, quieter alternative:

ABOVE Plotting a new Argentina under satin sheets: from *Evita* (1979), Eva Peron (Patti LuPone) cannot be, and will not be, and must not be denied.

There again we could be foolish not to quit while we're ahead
I can see us many miles away, inactive
Sipping cocktails on a terrace, taking breakfast in bed
Sleeping easy, doing nothing, it's attractive.

To Eva, such pleasant thoughts are "nightmares" that "always take some swallowing." On her terrace, she'd much prefer singing power ballads to sipping cocktails, and, indeed, the first-act closer, "Don't Cry for Me, Argentina," represents the culmination of decades of glamorous ladies being celebrated by the chorus. Evita gets to have an entire working-class populace as her backup chorus, each one lustily chanting her name.

As far as being a leading lady in a Broadway musical goes, does that beat sipping cocktails and taking breakfast in bed? It all depends on whether you want to be powerfully drunk—like Vera Charles—or, like Eva Peròn, drunk with power.

THE CORNHUSKER OR MAME'S MINT JULEP

(Inspired by *Mame*, 1966)

◇

"You give my old mint julep a kick—Mame!"

What exactly was the kick that Mame brought to this classic American drink? Hard to know, other than an inspiration to be indomitable. The mint julep has existed in some form or another since the middle of the eighteenth century, and it has evolved into a delectation with a distinctly Southern pride of place.

SILVER MINT JULIP GLASS OR HIGHBALL + MUDDLER

Cracked ice

3 ounces bourbon (your choice)

10 sprigs fresh mint, for muddling; you can include stalks

1 teaspoon finely granulated sugar

1 splash seltzer

1 stalk mint, 6–7 inches long, to garnish

Fill your glass three-quarters full with the cracked ice and refrigerate. While the glass is chilling, strip the leaves from the sprigs of fresh mint and place them in a mixing glass. Sprinkle the sugar on top. Add the seltzer and muddle until the mint flavor is released. Next, add the bourbon. Stir gently with a bar spoon, then strain into your chilled glass. Twirl your spoon elegantly to make sure the ice and liquor are mixed, until you can see the outside of the glass begin to frost, but be careful not to touch the glass with warm hands—use a towel. Garnish with the stalk of mint.

— GET THAT ICE —

The easiest way to crack ice is to put the ice into a 1-gallon plastic bag and smack the bag with a mallet or thick wooden spoon. Some bartenders put the ice in a towel and bash it against the counter, but I find the ice often sticks to cloth material. Don't worry if the ice is irregularly shaped—it's aesthetically pleasing in this context.

THE SAZERAC

(Inspired by *State of the Union*, 1945)

The Sazerac is a classic and thoroughly satisfying drink born out the flavors and tastes of New Orleans. It's also the only cocktail I know of that has its own recipe written into the dialogue of a play (and spelled slightly differently):

SPIKE (to SWENSON, the hired bartender): *Do you know how to mix a Sazarac?*

SWENSON: *No, but I can look it up.*

SPIKE: *Well, I'll tell you. Take an old-fashioned glass and put a lump of sugar in it, soaked in Pernod. Then a jigger of bourbon, a twist of lemon peel on top, and give it a good stir. Don't sample that one, Swenson, it'll light up your vest buttons.*

In the film, Spike (played by Van Johnson) adds that the drink is "absolute suicide." When Lulubelle Alexander asks Swenson if he knows how to make one, he replies, "I think so." She turns to her husband and declares, authoritatively, "If he just thinks so, Jeff, you'd better mix that Sazarac."

The Sazerac also happens to be this author's favorite cocktail. Here's a more refined recipe:

OLD FASHIONED
+ ATOMIZER

1 teaspoon simple syrup (or ½ teaspoon finely granulated sugar mixed with water)

3 ounces rye (spring for a nice one, if you can)

Dash Peychaud's bitters

1 lemon peel (optional)

2 sprays of absinthe (or Absente or Pernod)

Pour the simple syrup (or sugar mixture, if you want a rougher residue) in the glass. Swirl the liquid around the inside of the glass and discard any that is left over. Add a large ice cube. Pour in the rye, add a dash of Peychaud's, rub the lemon peel around the rim of the glass, then drop it in, if you so choose. Swirl the mixture gently, but authoritatively, in your hand. Use an atomizer to spray the absinthe on top of the drink at least two times, but no more than four. That would be absolute suicide.

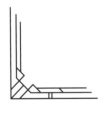

THE ANNIE WARBUCKS

(Inspired by *Annie*, 1977)

◇

A drink based on the indomitable Annie Warbucks must have some bite to it and not devolve into the sticky sweet concoctions usually associated with "kiddie cocktails." There's no good reason for young adults to sit with long, resentful faces watching the adults have a good time at a cocktail party; nor does one need to embarrass them by referring to a "kiddie cocktail." You can make a perfectly refreshing non-alcoholic drink that makes your young guests stick out their chins and grin.

Ginger is a key ingredient—in the form of ginger beer—because Annie is a redhead, and the orange ingredients pick up on her comic-strip hair color. The Tamarind syrup is a nod to Punjab, Daddy Warbucks's loyal bodyguard from the Far East who appeared in the comic strip about a decade in and provided multitudes of adventure; the stage musical, unaccountably, left him out, but the 1982 movie allowed him an appearance at least.

CLEAR GLASS
COFFEE MUG*

2 teaspoons tamarind syrup (or tamarind molasses)

12 ounce can ginger beer (despite the name, it's non-alcoholic; I like Fever-Tree)

2 teaspoons orange juice

2 orange slices (optional)

1 straw

Put a few ice cubes in the mug. Add the tamarind syrup
(which can be quite sticky), then the orange juice and ginger beer. Stir gently.
If you're feeling up to it, cut two small orange slices for garnish around the rim.
Do those resemble Annie's pupil-less eyes from the comic strip? Maybe.
Serve the drink with a straw, and, if you don't think it will spoil your
youngster, bring the drink in on a tray. When they're through,
perhaps Mrs. Pugh comes and takes it away?

* IF YOU HAVE A LITTLE ORPHAN ANNIE SHAKE-UP MUG LYING AROUND, WELL USE THAT, OF COURSE.

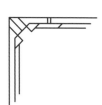

THE PINK LADY

(Inspired by *Grease*, 1972)

◇

The Pink Lady has a real cocktail as its provenance, a cocktail that was not only popular in the early part of the twentieth century, but may also be the first cocktail named after a Broadway show. *The Pink Lady* was a 1911 Edwardian operetta imported from England to Broadway's New Amsterdam Theatre, where it ran an impressive (for the time) 312 performances. Apparently, the show's songs fit into the narrative with more integrity than most musical productions of the era.

The show's leading lady, Hazel Dawn, claimed the drink had been concocted in her honor at a party at Murray's Roman Gardens on 42nd Street. According to the *Oxford Companion to Spirits & Cocktails*, the cocktail was tagged as a "ladies' drink"—i.e., something no red-blooded American male would dare order, even though the cocktail was far more potent than the usual rounds routinely ordered by male customers in manly tones at bars across America.

So, the idea that the Pink Lady would put hair on your chest—theoretically speaking, of course—seems like exactly the kind of challenge that would appeal to Betty Rizzo and her gang.

**COUPE
+ COCKTAIL SHAKER**

1 egg white
2 ounces gin
2 ounces calvados

Juice ½ lime
1 tablespoon grenadine
Cracked ice (see p. 159)

Chill the glass by putting it in the freezer for 5 minutes. Separate an egg white
by gently splitting a raw egg in half over a small bowl, let the white drip into
the bowl while shifting the yolk back and forth from shell to shell.
Pour the egg white, gin, calvados, lime juice, and grenadine into a cocktail shaker. Add
ice, then shake vigorously. Strain the cocktail into the chilled glass.
It may seem counterintuitive to add an egg white to
such a potent draught, but, trust me, these ingredients go together
like rama-lama-lama-ka-dinga-da-dinga-dong.

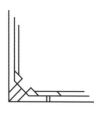

THE LOVERLY

(Inspired by *My Fair Lady*, 1956)

"Nobody ever saw the sign of liquor on me," retorts Eliza Doolittle to one of Henry Higgins's more insensitive remarks, early in *My Fair Lady*. In this regard, Eliza's abstemiousness neatly parallels that of the musical's progenitor, George Bernard Shaw, whose 1912 play *Pygmalion* (and the subsequent 1938 cinematic adaptation) is the source material for the musical. Shaw, an early advocate and factotum of Socialism in the late-nineteenth century, saw temperance as an important value in building a society of men and women who were healthy and resilient. "Alcohol is the anesthesia by which we endure the operation of life," he once wrote. That may be why the play and musical's major figure of fun is Eliza's father, Alfred Doolittle, a "common dustman" who is not only a jolly inebriate, but also the text's most eloquent explicator on the hypocrisy of middle-class morality.

Nonetheless, Eliza is capable of temptation, but of a much gentler kind: chocolate. To get her to listen to his proposal of an experiment to transform her into a passable duchess at an embassy ball, Higgins brandishes a box of chocolates: "You shall have boxes of them, barrels of them, every day. You shall live on them, eh?"

Since Eliza transformed admirably, it seems only fair to build a cocktail around "lots of choc'late." It's loverly, it is.

MARTINI
+COCKTAIL SHAKER

2 ounces vodka

1 ounce Godiva dark chocolate liqueur

1 ounce white crème de cacao

1 chocolate bon-bon (your choice)

Combine the vodka, chocolate liqueur, and crème de cacao in a cocktail shaker. Add ice. Place a bon-bon at the bottom of the glass, then strain the cocktail into the glass. (To make the drink even more special, grind up a bit of your favorite chocolate, then before placing the bonbon in the glass, wet the rim and dip it in the chocolate to coat.) Once you've finished drinking, you can break the bon-bon in half, take one part, and share the other half with a guest, just as Higgins did with Eliza: "A pledge of good faith."

RAINBOW HIGH OR THE EVITA MARGARITA

(Inspired by *Evita*, 1979)

Eva Peron went to great—some might say "excessive"—lengths to create a new Argentina for her *descamisados*, but one thing she was never able to give them was a national cocktail.

This is a bit strange, as most large countries in Central and Latin America have their own distinctive national drink—cachaça in Brazil, pisco in Chile (and Peru), tequila in Mexico—but Argentina seems to have gone without such fermented associations. What passes for a national drink is Coca-Cola laced with a Milan-based digestif called Fernet-Branca. Fernet-Branca has been around for two centuries, a viscous motor-oil-brown-colored bitters with a secret recipe. It's not for the faint-of-heart, but then neither was Evita.

This cocktail doesn't have a rainbow of colors but it is inspired by Evita's eternal desire to rise above the quotidian and make an impression. These days, margaritas come in all shapes and sizes (and flavors and colors), but, for my money, less is more. This particular recipe is bracing in the way Eva herself was and it promotes a bit of local color.

OLD FASHIONED + COCKTAIL SHAKER

3 ounces tequila (100% agave)

1 ounce Pierre Ferrand dry curaçao

Juice ½ lime

1 tablespoon Fernet-Branca

Cracked ice (see p. 159)

Add the cracked ice to a cocktail shaker. Pour in the tequila, curacao, and lime juice. Shake well, then strain into an old-fashioned glass. Add more ice, if the weather is warm, or if you just like a cold cocktail. Pour the Fernet-Branca over the top. It's not one's usual sweet trifle, but it would be surprisingly good for you.

102

ABOUT THE AUTHOR

———————◇———————

Laurence Maslon is an arts professor at New York University's Tisch School of the Arts, as well as associate chair of the Graduate Acting Program. His most recent book is an updated companion volume to the PBS series *Broadway: The American Musical*. He is also the host and producer of the weekly radio series, *Broadway to Main Street* (winner of the 2019 ASCAP Foundation/Deems Taylor Award for Radio Broadcast) on the NPR station WLIW-FM. He edited the two-volume set *American Musicals* (1927-1969) for Library of America, as well as their *Kaufman & Co.*, Broadway comedies by George S. Kaufman. Other books include the companion book to *Come From Away*, *Broadway to Main Street: How Show Music Enchanted America* (Oxford), *The Sound of Music Companion*, and the *South Pacific Companion*. He is the writer and coproducer of the PBS American Masters documentary, *Sammy Davis, Jr.: I've Gotta Be Me*, and wrote American Masters documentary *Richard Rodgers: The Sweetest Sounds*. He served on the nominating committee for the Tony Awards from 2007 to 2010. He has written for *The New York Times*, *The Washington Post*, the *New Yorker*, *Opera News*, *Stagebill*, and *American Theatre*. Mr. Maslon, otherwise a nice guy, mixes a mean drink.

ABOUT THE PHOTOGRAPHER

———————◇———————

Joan Marcus is one of the preeminent theatrical photographers working in the US today. Over the past 25 years she has photographed more than 500 shows on and off Broadway and regionally. A native of Pittsburgh, Pennsylvania, Joan graduated from George Washington University. In 2014 she received a Tony Honor for Excellence in the Theater.

PREVIOUS SPREAD Phil Silvers is either being given the best seat in the Casacabana nightclub--or being tossed out. Either is possible in the 1960 Styne-Comden-Green musical *Do Re Mi*.

ACKNOWLEDGMENTS

First, I have to raise a glass to Karyn Gerhard, the Toast of Bedford. Given the effervescent nature of our previous collaborations, it seems only fitting that this book should be the first new book for her to edit at Weldon Owen. I'm honored and look forward to many more.

I have to order another round to toast photographer Joan Marcus. Any one of the thousands of theatrical folk who have come under Joan's spell (or under her lens) knows that she embodies everything that's fun and vital and specific about the joy of the theater. We first met in the little village of Arena Stage in another century, so it's a particular thrill to have collaborated with her on the photos for this book; she makes the cocktails sing and dance on their own, don't you think?

The good folks at Sardi's were so gracious and accommodating during Joan's shoots of our cocktail recipes that the little I can do in recompense is to show the world how special Sardi's is as a theatrical landmark through Joan's amazing photos. Special kudos to Max Klimamvicius.

For our photo shoots, we had the support and eagle eye of Amy Klein and Genevieve Elam. Genevieve, in particular, passed judgment on every cocktail in this book; she comes by it honestly—we shared them before dinner most nights of the week. Other chums who contributed their company over drinks include Lewis J. Stadlen, Jay Wegman, Matthew Sussman, Stephanie Janssen, Britian Siebert, Jacob Orr, Mary Claire Hogan, Fritz Brun, and the Mattituck gang.

Doug Reside at the New York Public Library, Lauren Robinson at MCNY, Dr. Edward Burns at the Carl Van Vechten Trust, Jennifer Bello Roberts at the Halsman Trust, and Todd Ifft at Photofest were indispensable in getting the archival photos together and a bend of the elbow to Ian Belknap and Dean Allyson Green for their assistance.

Steve Ross, the VSOP of literary agents, demonstrated the high proof of his skills and acumen and Charles Kopelman, that rare vintage of theatrical agents, provided his usual unwavering support.

Anyone else who may have inadvertently omitted, the next one is on me.

> ### DEDICATION
> To Eileen and Linus,
> Cami and Tim, and
> Tracey and Albert,
> the R&D wing of this enterprise.
> *Amigos*, together!

PHOTO CREDITS

◇

Every effort has been made to acknowledge correctly and contact the source and/or copyright holder for each image in this book. Any errors or omissions are unintentional and will be corrected in future editions.

weldon**owen**

an imprint of Insight Editions
P.O. Box 3088
San Rafael, CA 94912
www.weldonowen.com

CEO Raoul Goff
VP Publisher Roger Shaw
Editorial Director Katie Killebrew
Senior Editor Karyn Gerhard
VP Creative Chrissy Kwasnik
Art Director and Designer Allister Fein
VP Manufacturing Alix Nicholaeff
Sr Production Manager Joshua Smith
Sr Production Manager, Subsidiary Rights
Lina s Palma-Temena

Weldon Owen would also like to thank Margaret Parrish and
Jon Ellis for their stellar work on this project.

Text © 2023 Laurence Maslon

ISBN: 978-1-68188-965-8

Manufactured in China by Insight Editions
10 9 8 7 6 5 4 3 2 1

ROOTS of PEACE   REPLANTED PAPER

Insight Editions, in association with Roots of Peace, will plant two
trees for each tree used in the manufacturing of this book. Roots
of Peace is an internationally renowned humanitarian organization
dedicated to eradicating land mines worldwide and converting
war-torn lands into productive farms and wildlife habitats. Roots
of Peace will plant two million fruit and nut trees in Afghanistan
and provide farmers there with the skills and support necessary for
sustainable land use.